AF882258

Alina Maria Șerban & Andreea Oana Șerban

eLAWvation

More Than a Lawyer

eLAWvate Yourself and Your Practice

This Book cannot and does not contain
[medical/legal/fitness/health/other] advice.
The [legal/medical/fitness/health/other] information
is provided for general informational and educational purposes only
and is not a substitute for professional advice.
Accordingly, before taking any actions based upon such information,
we encourage you to consult with the appropriate professionals. We do not
provide any kind of [medical/legal/fitness/health/other] advice.The use or
reliance of any information contained on this book is solely at your own risk.

www.elawvation.com

Legal Disclosures

All copyrights are reserved to the authors
Alina Maria Șerban and Andreea Oana Șerban

No part of this book can be reproduced or used, under any form, or purpose, through written or electronic means, including but not limited to photocopy, recording or any other means of storage or reproducing, without prior written approval.

Copyright © 2020, Alina Maria Șerban, Andreea Oana Șerban

ISBN (print) 978-1-7348907-1-6
ISBN (digital) 978-1-7348907-0-9

Table of Contents

A Different Argument for the Career of a Unique Lawyer

I have found myself reading the pages of this book through the uniqueness of a human being, as a divine gift. I think that this new goal of the *Unique Lawyer System* goes back to that professional of the universe of laws who knows how to rehabilitate the unique justice of the one he defends in relation to the legal system. Such a lawyer must be a good observer of the differences, the uniqueness of those around. In human terms, he will be successful in this task by relating to the justice system and facts.

I now invite you to dive into reading, enjoy the book!

Marian Șerban
(author's father)

Preface

It is a pleasure to express my thoughts on Andreea and Alina. The two lawyers worked very seriously to develop a business and a niche in Romania. And while working in the field they managed to continue their education in fields unrelated to law, to develop and create their lives as they wanted.

If you are a lawyer or a law-related professional, you must read this book – for several reasons. The authors of this book have a rich and long experience in the legal profession. They are unique: not just because they are identical twins and both work in the legal field, but also because they have courage, they show passion and creativity, qualities that have played a significant role in the search and creation of a new path in the thinking and profession of what it is to be a lawyer.

So, what is this path? It is one that many believe impossible and too far from reality for a lawyer to take seriously... although, precisely for that reason, maybe you should do it.

The research, time, and accuracy that Andreea and Alina have dedicated to writing this book is the foundation of a movement that legal professionals could benefit of – whether you just start your career, or you have been a lawyer for many years. Such a provocative work has never been published in a field that has remained traditional throughout history.

The concept is simple, but very powerful and has easy to follow and understand steps. The challenge for readers is related to enthusiasm and how they will be influenced – or not – in action and to become different.

There aren't many books that can change your life, but this one can! The question you must ask yourself is "Am I ready?" The fact that you are reading this now suggests that you are.

John Thompson,
Corporate Consultant,
Metropolis (author's coaching mentor)

Chapter 1
Unique and Different

We are all unique and different
And, thus, one can say we are alike…

The uniqueness is inherited
The difference is built

Chapter 1
Unique and different

The first steps on the Court's stairs. Downwards and upwards...

I remember like it has just happened today, the first time I walked up the stairs of a Courthouse. It was a summer day and I was an introverted girl; emotional and struggling with my inner battles. I remember all the small details, from what I was wearing (a white skirt and a red top) to the gentle touch of the sun on my face, my only witness to what I was truly feeling on the inside.

It was the day when my sister and I were going to Court to choose with whom we wanted to live after our parents' divorce. We were going up the stairs slowly, feeling like we were taking a step backwards with every step, and I was looking down, carrying an unspoken feeling of guilt as if I was responsible for what had happened. In all honesty, I felt somehow responsible for my parents' life.

Shy and emotional, at the top of the stairs I was welcomed by an unknown man. I recall every detail as if I am looking at his face now, a tall, harsh, and serious man and for a second everything froze around me. He asked me: "What do you want to become when you grow up?"

I felt a shiver deep within, my heart was chilled by the cold wind of his words, a leaf in the autumn breeze. I felt even more responsible, even more confused. On one hand, I was there to make a final decision for what my life was going to be like from that moment on as well as the life of my parents. On the other hand, I was treated like a child who did not know what she was going to do with her life but was being forced to make a "grownup decision". My sister and I were the ones to choose the verdict in a situation so complicated and harrowing for both our lives and our parents' lives. We were talking about destroying the dream of every child - to grow up with both parents. Looking back, this dream proved to be a sandcastle on which bitter waters dripped. It was our family...

I stood for a moment without breathing. I was trying to hold back my tears. Finally, with a voice that I didn't recognize, I said loudly and emphatically: "Lawyer! Lawyer. I'll become a lawyer when I grow up." I was looking right into the man's eyes. I thought he was the one stealing my mother from our nest. I felt a lot of anger, a rapid heartbeat and terrible pain. But more than that, I felt a great desire to do whatever it took to achieve this dream, which was sketched in a moment of suffering. It was a dream created from our pain, a dream created there, on the stairs of the courthouse.

It was the day that my sister and I chose whom we were going to live with. It was the day I recorded in my journal, the path for my future professional life. But it was also the day that my sister, Andreea, gave up her childhood dream: to become a fashion designer. Andreea stayed with me. Together we overcame the moments of grief and embarked on a new path, discovered back then, on the stairs of the court.

I wrote in my journal what my life as a lawyer would be like, down to the smallest details. I was going to become a successful lawyer and have my own law office. I was going to travel and speak many foreign languages.

Exactly ten years after that moment, I was in a red leather chair at my office, which made me feel important and fulfilled. It was the day my sister and I opened our own law office. It was the start of our career marathon. And it really was a marathon, because since day one I took everything seriously, with the utmost responsibility. We were working, studying, and looking for clients. It was just the two of us, and I was doing lawyer work and secretarial work. Everything until that day of August when our lives would change. Of course, we didn't know that yet, so we decided to leave for a week of vacation to Santorini in Greece.

We arrived in Athens, where, in two days, we would board a ship that would take us to the famous island of Santorini. During the trip, we received a call from a good friend who knew we were in Athens and asked if we wanted to meet with a lawyer who needed a consultation in Romania. I answered yes rather unconsciously, full of enthusiasm for a new beginning. It was the answer to the promise that we had made to ourselves on the stairs of the courthouse ten years before.

I didn't know this back then, but in time, I understood that when you say "yes" to something, you automatically say "no" to something else. Since we were on vacation, we did not have suitable clothes for an official meeting. We knew that in our profession, appearance is very important. Clothing must appear serious and sober (dark colors, no prints), with appropriate shoes, proper hairstyle, and attitude. We managed to quickly put this together.

The meeting was scheduled for the next day at 12 o'clock. It was our first meeting with a foreign lawyer and not just any lawyer. He was a renowned lawyer who worked for one of the most well-known law offices in Athens. We were going to one of the central streets of the Greek capital with timid steps, but every stone of the sidewalk framed by the orange blossoms gave us more courage.

When we arrived at the lawyer's office, we were invited into the conference room that was filled with only old wooden chairs — silent witnesses to countless histories and secrets. We heard, then, the firm footsteps that were headed to where we were. I felt a sense of serenity, as if everything was the natural outcome of the decisive moment since our parents' divorce.

We made our presentations with confidence. After answering several questions, the lawyer told us about an international legislative project that was to start in Romania. It was a part of the legislation that had never interested us. When he finished his speech, the Greek lawyer asked assertively if we would be interested in taking on this task and if we felt we would be good at doing such projects. Without looking at my sister, we said yes in unison, both full of confidence.

The foreign lawyer gave us the impression that he was happy to have found someone to solve his problem who, above all, is serious, conscientious and responsible.

The lawyer lit a cigarette and informed us that there might be a problem - the project had to be finished very quickly. "Could you manage to complete it by the end of the month?" he asked. For us to complete the project in a month, we would have to work intensely. Keep in mind that we had no experience in that field and we were at the beginning of our career. Still, we shook hands with the Greek lawyer without further questions or comments. He promised to send us an email with all the details and conditions of the collaboration that we had not discussed.

When we got out of the office, I felt the warmth of that summer day as I had never felt before. We looked at each other and said, "What do we do now? Go back home?" But the question was superfluous. We both knew that we would make the decision to give up our vacation for that project, and it turned out to be the beginning of our successful career. Here is how I turned down a vacation and won a career! I firmly decided, and I knew it was not a simple decision, but it was about something bigger, more important, I knew that even more was waiting around the corner.

Today, after another ten years, we are sitting on chairs in a circle, surrounded by colleagues. They are our colleagues at the Integrative Psychotherapy Training School. We are here to open our final Chambers, which were closed long ago. This is the time when we can finally re-evaluate our success and we can look back on all those years in the past when we climbed the stairs of the unknown and descended to the deepest states of self-profound awareness, but also to the hidden angels of our profession.

After much personal analysis and development, my sister and I have managed to discover and polish that diamond that every person has inside them. That is how this second book was born, which for us represents the fruit of the mission we took on: to share all those things that have brought us success, but also to offer ideas, techniques, and tools that really helped us on this road.

Thus, was born the *Unique Lawyer System.* A system accessible to any lawyer who wishes to make a difference not only in his or her life, but also in the lives of their clients. The goal is to live a more fulfilled life and to gain more without stress. We had the courage to create this system in 2011 after we launched the first project for lawyers, called *Lawyer Coaching*, both in Bucharest and in Milan. The testimonials of our clients who participated in the courses we organized gave us the resolve to start working on something far more advanced. This would evolve into *The Unique Lawyer System.* Today, my sister and I are practicing in Bucharest and Milan, and we continue to focus on coaching activities for lawyers, helping them implement this system in their profession, while working to eliminate issues that sabotage their work and implement strategies to help them become more successful.

In 2012, we published the book, *Unique and Different.* We decided to follow the courses of *Faculty of Psychology and Training in Integrative Psychotherapy.* We are very happy with this choice because we have always been passionate about observing and studying the human psyche.

We believe these investments in our personal development can be extremely beneficial to our legal profession. We considered that becoming lawyers did not equate to the employee status of the client, but rather with the person whom anyone can count on. As lawyers, we need to know how to be more than legal advisors. We need to be consultants and psychologists but above all, to be human.

We conceived this book as a guide to help others understand a Unique Lawyer model. It is written in order to help you make the most of the practice of this profession, in full accordance with your personal life.

Why "different"? Because it is about the lawyer who wants to make a difference, to differentiate himself or herself from others through everything that makes them unique. Have you ever wondered why some are successful and others are not? That is what we are talking about, both in our book and in our coaching activities.

The book is the result of our experience, both professionally and personally. Our hope is that by reading it, you can learn to operate your practice in a different way. Being a lawyer is just a part of your life, and the way you fulfill your professional role can cause pleasure or pain, it may be in your favor or it could work against you.

We trust that this book will help you enjoy your professional activity to a greater extent; that it can motivate you to give your best as a specialist, not only for the prospect of material gain, but also for your personal satisfaction. In the following chapters we will explain, step by step, some of the secrets of this profession and we will show you how we think it can be practiced in harmony with you and others.

The mission we propose is to challenge our fellow lawyers, however, this book can be a useful tool to specialists from other fields where working with people plays an essential role. The challenge is for the reader to become aware that before they are responsible for their clients, they must be responsible for the quality of their own lives, and consider parameters such as happiness, success, health or vitality and give them a model for activating their full potential.

Today, the society has a certain perception of the lawyer, influenced by preconceived ideas and behavior. This perception may distort individuals' image in public consciousness. We consider that a recovery of the image of the legal profession is extremely necessary, but the image itself should not be based solely on marketing strategies, but on real changes in the quality of the personal and professional life of the contemporary lawyer.

We had in our career a moment when we felt the need to stop and reboot our professional life, so we could enjoy the beneficial effects of this change also in our personal life.

We began noticing that our lives had become greatly enriched because we gained important elements such as:

- Feeling of physical and emotional well-being
- Strengthening relationships with close relatives
- Increasing the quality of our relationship with our clients
- The feeling of harmony and balance between personal and professional life
- The choice to develop our staff
- The chance to provide a sense of meaning to our lives
- The pleasure of professional practice as a lawyer
- Creating a pleasant work environment
- Satisfaction from clients, colleagues, and collaborators
- And, last but not least, personal satisfaction

We understand how important it is not to start this journey alone. Any change is possible when we unite our efforts in a certain direction. That is why we are trying to share the result of our experiences with our readers in order to encourage them to move forward with confidence on the path of becoming a Unique Lawyer.

Most lawyers manage to achieve outstanding results for the causes they represent and strive to fulfill all the obligations they have agreed to on behalf their clients. However, it often demands too high a price on their personal life, their health, and even their families. By applying the methods and steps we are about to reveal, we believe that you can create and maintain a balance between your personal and professional life.

Now, we invite you to become a member of *The Unique Lawyer System* to enter the club of lawyers who make a difference, both in their personal lives and in relation to their clients. When you dedicate yourself to the profession with calm, relaxation and confidence, the solutions appear much faster.

It has been shown that maximum efficiency in any professional environment is achieved in terms of maintaining a state of calm. A successful professional focus on solving a single problem, staying focused on it and prioritizing with the confidence that he will solve the other matters at the right time, in the best manner for everyone.

We will discuss how we communicate, how we organize our calendar, how we address our clients, how we can widen our circle of clientele and, last but not least, how we find and maintain our emotional balance that gives us the right perspective on life, so that we have the feeling of value and personal fulfillment, regardless of professional challenges.

We hope that the lawyers who read this book will find a favorable framework for

self-discovery and personal development, so that their lives will be filled with balance, success and fulfillment. You will have the methods and practices of a successful lawyer at your fingertips. We are ready to share them with you in the pages of this book.

Before Choosing to Become a Lawyer

What do you really want in life? Are you on the path you really want? Are you confused, even though you may have wanted to be a lawyer for many years? Whether you are at the beginning of the road or have years of rich experience, you can face a sense of insecurity in terms of the road you are following. The first step is to ask yourself what you really want in life.

Of course, becoming aware of your own desires and acknowledging the point where you are currently on the path to achieving your own ideals, does not ensure easy and direct access to the proposed goal. It takes a lot of effort, determination and capacity to organize and regulate work.

And, there is no doubt, it takes a lot of courage. The courage to examine and critically analyze yourself, to break down your negative qualities and faults into pieces that you can honestly explore and then rebuild yourself into the best possible version. In other words, get to know yourself better so that you can achieve more from life, both in personal and professional ways.

People generally want:

- A beautiful, healthy and dynamic life, free of problems
- To feel healthy and comfortable in their own body
- To have more vitality
- More balance between work and personal life
- A successful career
- Happiness in personal relationships
- Health for their children
- To enjoy life more
- Have friends, travel and have fun
- Have a good financial situation

For this purpose, we propose that you try to answer fundamental questions like the following:

- Who am I really and why am I here?
- Where do I want to get and why?
- What is the purpose of my life?
- How do I get there?
- What are the barriers in my life that keep me from reaching the success I want?
- At this moment of my life, am I on the right track?
- How will I feel when I reach my goal?
- How will I benefit when I meet my goal?
- What will my life be like when I achieve my goal?

Your personal evaluation based on past experiences will lead you to questions about the profession, implicitly:

- Does the profession of being a lawyer match my skills and goals?
- If not, why not, and what can I do to change this?
- What is blocking me from successfully practicing as a lawyer?
- What keeps me stuck (family situation, friends, beliefs, fears)?
- Do I feel stressed about practicing law? What can I do about this?
- What is most important to me about this profession?
- Why do I want to be a lawyer?
- What does this profession offer me, apart from financial gain?
- What are my personal benefits if I choose to be a lawyer?
- How can this profession help me grow personally?
- What do I like about this profession?

Once you have answered these questions, you should have an overview of the situation you are in.

We will now continue with the next exercise. It is important that during your reading, you have a clear idea of where you are and where you want to go. Try to answer these questions before you continue to read through the pages of this book. You will benefit more from this exercise if you write down your answers. This type of evaluation assists the thinking processes to help you draw up a plan in order to have as much professional and personal satisfaction as possible.

DO I REALLY WANT TO BECOME A LAWYER?

It is a question that can be difficult to answer. Some people claim to have known since childhood that they wanted to embrace this profession, but others have fought this decision until they applied for law school. In fact, many law students and even those who have recently graduated from law schools are still unsure of the answer to this question.

It is difficult to have a definitive answer, but we can offer some useful suggestions to help you gain a better understanding of the world of the professional lawyer. Before deciding to apply for a seat in law school, it would probably be beneficial to talk to practitioners, participate in civil and criminal trials, and attend a few law courses. These steps can give you more information about what a lawyer does. However, these methods can only provide superficial ideas without really being able to capture the multiple challenges, complexity, difficulty and demands of this profession. By sharing this information, we try to take a look behind the scenes of this career, revealing a different view of the profession.

The process of deciding about choosing this career can also be distorted by the difficulty of defining what a lawyer does day by day. There's no model of a typical lawyer. Today, the attorney profession offers the choice between several specializations. Depending on the chosen specialization (criminal law, family law, commercial litigation, real estate, trade and commercial litigation, tax legislation, labor law, environmental law, patent and trademark law, human rights legislation, etc.), there will be differences between workload, how to contact clients, work environment, income, and quality of life.

We strongly believe that a significant way to determine if you want to dedicate yourself to this career is to analyze the type of traits that one must develop to eventually become a competent lawyer. Although there are significant differences in many areas of law practice, the essential skills required for any lawyer are roughly the same.

Think about how you would honestly answer the following questions:

1 Do I enjoy working closely with people, taking part in significant events or problems affecting their lives?

Invariably, lawyers are involved in people's lives. This involvement can be by way of one-on-one communication, a meeting, or through legal documents. You will need to feel comfortable and safe with the fact that your advice, your counseling, along with all other actions, will have a significant impact on your clients' lives. *The Unique Lawyer System* will use additional tools to manage these relationships, giving you the ability to identify client issues that are often difficult and emotionally challenging.

2 Can I empathize with a client's situation and still have the ability to objectively analyze his problems and consequences, according to the applicable laws?

The main task of a lawyer is to solve the client's problem. People are asking him or her for help to solve their legal issues. A lawyer must be able to empathize in order to properly understand the client's needs and worries. He must objectively develop analytical skills in order to identify possible legal viewpoints that need to be addressed. Then he has to formulate a plan to reach a consistent result which includes the client's wishes and to follow legal requirements. *The Unique Lawyer System* will develop his ability to empathize, but also the ability to detach. Empathy is necessary to understand the client's reality, which is also the starting point in building the best strategy for the particular situation.

3 Can I explain the legal reality to my clients? Am I able to present reality objectively, even if the person in front of me chooses to see it from a subjective perspective?

We live in a complex society, which requires development and elaboration of appropriate laws. It goes without saying that most clients will be incompletely informed of the law in force or will have significant misunderstandings on what the law permits or prohibits. A lawyer must be able to educate his clients on these aspects. This act of bringing the legal reality to the forefront can prove more difficult because the client is directly involved in the debated subject. The degree or understanding will be affected by your own legitimate interest, the lack of desire to hear the bad news, and a strong disagreement on the objectives of unfavorable law.

The need to educate is critical from the acceptance perspective of a well-informed decision from the client. Tact is absolutely necessary to be able to tell a client that his or her vision of the applicable laws in a certain case is erroneous. A Unique Lawyer will understand the need to grasp these subtle different communication techniques.

4 Am I able to convey my analysis of a problem to others in a clear and concise way, whether in written or verbally?

We believe that a good lawyer should have two vital abilities: to speak and to write clearly and concisely. Since a lawyer's duty is to solve the legal issues of his clients, the key to success lies in his ability to make himself credible by convincing others of the correctness of his problem analysis. Of course, this analysis will be developed within the framework described by the boundaries of the law. The lawyer will look for the best solution for his client within those limits.

To give his clients a win, an effective lawyer will successfully play the persuasive role towards his clients and the parties involved in the judicial process: other lawyers, judges, mediators, prosecutors, etc. The lawyer must have the capability to achieve this part of the communication as well, both verbally and in written, being aware that this is a fundamental part of his professional activity, which overwhelmingly entails working with people.

You may be a genius, but that will not do you much good in this job, if others cannot understand what you are saying. Competence in the art of verbal communication is an important key in your effort to become a successful lawyer.

5 Am I happy in exercising my legal profession? Can I argue both sides of a problem with my client showing the same enthusiasm?

We believe that the personal satisfaction of a lawyer must find its source in the approach of helping others achieve the desired results or avoid (or possibly minimize) the consequences of a difficult situation. A lawyer must provide the client with sufficient information regarding all possible legal options to enable him to take a decision appropriate to his/her needs. It is important to note that the client is the one who needs to decide what is best for him when it comes to his own business or his future. The lawyer must be able to accept his decision and represent him even if the lawyer himself would not have made that choice. However, the attorney must be sure that the decision falls within the legal parameters.

Whether it is about negotiating a contract, judging a lawsuit or settling a divorce, the lawyer pleads for the personal needs, desires and objectives of the client. To excel in his profession, a lawyer does not need to be liked. He only needs to be able to convincingly support the strategy he chose in front of the client.

6 Do I like to focus on the details? Do I like to get involved completely - to look for the concrete facts of a situation?

If you choose to only focus on the problems you can see on the surface, as legal practice can be a puzzle with invisible parts. You will never solve the whole issue unless you are ready to get involved with the necessary energy and determination it takes to solve a particular problem. The lawyer must pay special attention to the facts and details, because details are a significant aspect of practicing the law. We do not want to say that you have to get lost in the details, but they must guide you in looking for the most suitable solutions.

7 Do I have a constant appetite for knowledge? Do I like to read, study, and document information?

For a lawyer, the study of normative acts and legal topics never ceases. Moreover, a lawyer needs information from various specialized areas, which can help him make the necessary associations in concrete causes. From the first day you enter law school and until the day you retire, it is advisable to not only keep up with the changes in the law but also with what is happening in the world.

Whether it's regulation or jurisprudence, you'll soon notice how counterproductive it can be to assume that the law is static. On a regular basis, each lawyer must dedicate a significant number of hours to update his knowledge. This time can be added on top of many hours of study spent in front of the computer, conducting research on specific issues of law, which are a part of particular cases.

The Unique Lawyer System will therefore be involved in your personal development. These are some of the ways that you can stay current: either by attending classes, workshops, or studying these themes, reading and information gathering. You will manage to better handle your relationship with yourself and also the relationship with your clients.

8 Am I able to relate well with people? Do I enjoy talking with them to find out their problems so that I can help them?

A lawyer has to deal with a large number of people. It is precisely for this reason that we have chosen to write this book: as an invitation for the attorney to know his own needs in order to recognize the needs of others; to provide others with help in solving their legal problems. We understand that any lawyer should first be a good psychologist. They should be interested first and foremost in the client in front of him, and his needs, and only then in the problems of a legal nature.

Now that we have reached the end of our questions, I want you to look back over them and see how many questions you answered with Yes. Did you answer yes enthusiastically, or did you need time to think about them?

In order to be a competent lawyer, it is not necessary to have all these abilities from the outset, but it is important to show the willingness to acquire them during your career. You will be able to develop them gradually by using all these skills weekly, daily or even hourly in your professional activity. Be aware that they are an essential part of the life of a lawyer.

You have heard the saying "truth is stranger than fiction" many times and maybe you have experienced it on your own. It is true that a career in the legal field can often hold you in suspense, even more than cinematic fiction. But the everyday life of a lawyer is not always taken out of a Hollywood film. Televised documentaries about lawyers may have some basis in the truth, however, because the practice of law can certainly be captivating, meaningful and rewarding.

You will have the opportunity to positively influence the lives of many people throughout your career. You will get in contact with many people through events and moving in areas that you otherwise would not have had the opportunity to experience in your personal life. By practicing law, you will be able to build a vast amount of experience and educate yourself.

Legal practice is not for lethargic people or for those who always watch the clock. Being a lawyer is a continuous life experience that does not end when you leave the office or the courtroom. This life will constantly solicit you. Therefore, your attitude concerning life and work is very important. In other words, you have to be a person who genuinely loves to study, to document, and one who strives to offer the best professional practice.

Lawyers and doctors are similar.
When something hurts, we call a doctor
and when there is an injustice, we call an attorney.

**Most of us have called a doctor when complications arise
and a lawyer when we cannot solve a legal problem.**

We are part of a larger world,
living with our fellow people

**And the greatest urgency
is to morally recover ourselves.**

You Are Unique and Different

In our book, *Unique and Different*, we explain how we believe that each of us is unique, unrepeatable, different from any other human being.

Each person has his own life and his own rhythm; so, depending on how you are structured, you can create and maintain a balance in your life tailored to you. We can help you through the methods and techniques we present to you, but their application depends on you. There is no specific recipe. It is important to monitor yourself and find out when you felt the best and when you had the best results. We have often applied, in turn, this introspection process and we have drawn very beneficial conclusions for our professional life – but also personal – subsequently. Even so, we recommend that you continuously revise your inner exploration strategies. Why? Because, simply, our life represents a continuous transformation: what worked for me five years ago or even last year, today may be different, and then I will need another rhythm and different resources. The central idea is that we must progress, both in our personal and professional life.

The Life of a Unique Lawyer

Most of us have heard, before embracing this career, that law is an independent profession which gives you freedom of movement and the opportunity to create your own schedule as you please. In reality, I do not know how many of us have this luxury.

From the perspective of *The Unique Lawyer System*, have your way would mean, first of all, to manage or take care of ourselves. In order to be able to perform at peak efficiency, we must put ourselves at the top of our priority list. We must get enough rest, eat properly, exercise, and spend quality time with our family. This way, we can avoid feelings of guilt and frustration that are often encountered in the lives of busy and active people.

We believe that the essence of the activity of *The Unique Lawyer System* lies in the option to conduct your profession with conscience. Law is a profession subjected to the test of psychic pressures; pressures that come from all sides, with each problem one after another, with each client following the previous one.

Therefore, we believe that, besides professional responsibility, a lawyer must have the capacity and training necessary to cope with a diversity of emotional expressions from his clients.

In their professional activity, lawyers have different types of clients. But from our experience, we found that in life nothing is random. Each lawyer attracts a certain type of client: the one with which they resonate the most. So more or less complicated situations and more or less difficult clients are drawn according to a certain inner profile of each practicing attorney.

In our case, we have been able to observe this phenomenon since the beginning of our careers. We are twin sisters who practice law together, however, it cannot be said that we have had similar cases. One of us has dealt with clients with less complicated matters, while the other had clients who appealed to her services that had very serious conflicts. We both have to deal with the professional details of a case, but there is also work on the human side, particularly those that are dissatisfied with the judicial process.

I have met many colleagues who do not consider this to be an issue. The most incited pretext that I heard from other lawyers was that, in everyday practice, their interest does not focus on the client as a person, but as a way to make money and nothing more. From our point of view, this cold dissociation is not appropriate. On the contrary, addressing things from the perspective of combining the bureaucratic side with client testimonials, you can be much more effective.

Of course, each person is unique and behaves according to their way of thinking, but we want to emphasize that everyone can put a little effort towards optimizing their relationship skills in order to work better with others.

The Unique Lawyer, from our perspective, is that lawyer who does not allow himself to be "stolen" by the profession and who is constantly interested in the human side of the relationship with his clients, focusing on optimizing communication with them.

In all my years as a law professional, I have concluded that what matters most is to feel at peace with your conscience. Do not make the problems of the clients your problems and do not bring those problems home. This is easy to say, but hard to do! It is impossible to resist looking for solutions to a problem when you practice your profession with passion.

You will find, in your professional practice, that you often have the opportunity to enjoy the freedom of managing your own calendar. Therefore, you must take advantage of the freedom to organize your own life. We have structured this book in such a way that, for each phase of your career, (also for each stage of your personal life), we present tools designed to help you operate your profession, while ensuring a healthy balance between your personal and professional life.

As a lawyer advises his client to avoid a lawsuit when it is not in his best interest, we also want to offer you a practical guide to prevent a failure in your personal life. In managing the time allocated to the fragile balance between their professional and personal plans, most people believe that the right time will come to deal with their personal life but find that there are too many problems to be solved at the office that take priority.

We do not know any lawyer with a successful practice who does not confess that he has had or still has days when he leaves the office at 11 pm or at midnight and will resume working once they get home. This practice does not translate into productivity or efficiency.

What, at first, may seem like the expression of a high yield, will prove to be, in fact, a boomerang-effect habit. Everything pays off, but sooner or later, you have to know when to say "STOP". Eventually, if you don't say "stop" to a counterproductive practice, life will say "stop" to you in one way or another.

How can you organize your professional and personal life so that you can prevent the cultivation of bad habits like this from the outset? We believe that the solution lies in better self-knowledge and in the awareness of your own uniqueness. The fact is that the solutions and answers are all yours.

Be unique in your profession. This is the only way you will make a difference!

Fortunately, we live in a society that aims to encourage the pluralism of ideas. That's why people will always share different concepts with each other. But we can all agree on one thing at least: that our world is very different from the world in which our parents or grandparents lived. And that this continuing reinvention rate is accelerating, so most likely our children and grandchildren will live in a world that we can barely imagine today. We live and work in a dynamic, constantly changing world - in a society that challenges us to overcome the narrow boundaries of a particular profession. A world that challenges us every moment, a world that makes you constantly reinvent yourself, to be creative and innovative. How are we going to cope?

More specifically, in the context of an increasing number of lawyers and more law firms, what can make you unique? How can you distinguish yourself in a professional environment that is becoming more and more competitive?

Our goal is to share our wisdom to support others on their professional journey, and also use the knowledge and self-development that we have cultivated over the years and offer you some suggestions that we believe can contribute to your unique character in the professional context.

1. Give value and importance to every client

People do not suffer most from lack of love, but lack of significance. When you establish the way of working with one client or another, remember that the most important thing is to pay the same amount and quality of attention to everyone. The client wants to feel that his problem is the priority for you. After a chat with you, as his lawyer, he must feel special.

How can you achieve this? First impressions really matter: give him your full attention from the moment you receive him in the office until he walks out the door.

Address him by his name. Inform yourself about the company he represents and/or about him as a person and use the information collected in the preliminary discussions when considering the problem in question. This shows interest and appreciation.

Adopt an open and friendly attitude. Often, compassion is needed when it comes to less pleasant matters, but we will talk more extensively about this topic in the chapter on Managing Emotions.

Create a cozy, comfortable environment that inspires trust so that the client feels welcomed. I remember how, many times, clients entering our office have mentioned their first impression. You can basically prove, by your approach, that every client is important to you.

2. Be believable

I have always known we must offer value before we start billing. Lawyers often act as if they are fully convinced that every minute is paid. Of course, it is not ethical to stall, since people expect you to have solutions to their legal problems. But from our first year of practice, I have found that it is not advisable to give a solution at the first meeting (as, very often we did, and it was not the best solution). Help the client understand that you are ready and that you have the tools and the knowledge you need to engage in the case. Offer examples of similar cases that you have successfully solved. You can also show publications about certain situations that are related to the case.

Once you have earned your credibility in the eyes of your clients or potential clients, we recommend that you carefully monitor this image capital that you have worked for diligently. It is best to try not to be late for meetings and to respect your commitments.

3. Be generous

Your professional relationship with every client, you have worked for, is an important addition to your client portfolio. Try to encourage repeated business. Do not forget that a satisfied client brings in other clients. Email each client legislative news related to his field of business. Any valuable information will be appreciated. This practice conveys the idea that you appreciate the collaborative relationship you have and that you want to be helpful. There may have been fees for providing legislative information before, but today, access to information is much easier to access for anyone with the internet, so be smart and collect useful information for your clients. Send them in an email or even a newsletter titled: "Legal Tips from Office X"... etc.

4. Create advantages for your clients

Beyond communicating with your client on the case itself, you will have much to gain in the long run if you know how to manage the interpersonal relationship established when they first walked into your office. Based on the information you have been able to gather about your client, if you have the opportunity, propose to them, a collaboration with other clients or facilitate any business relationship that might be beneficial to them. Do it discreetly, respecting confidential data. Act with tact and intelligence. It is good to know, however, that you cannot begin such initiatives unless you feel that your professional and human relationship allows you to do so.

5. Be active and cultivate a social life. Participate in a business network.

This part of the attorney profession has been a great investment in our career. We have strived to be present at all kinds of public meetings related to our domain. You cannot wait for your clients to hire you just because you put a nice name above the office entrance and that's it.

Social relationships are fundamental. However, it is important not to ad dress this dimension of your professional activity as a prerequisite, because this way you will be exhausted very quickly. First, check the events related to your domain, make a list and organize your calendar according to their importance. Do not let this good habit turn into a routine obligation, don't exhaust yourself or become apathetic. At one point I had this feeling when I attended too many conferences and saw the same patterns; the same people who were just showing up. I felt like we were wasting our energy. Everything needs to be balanced by priorities and objectives. Determine where it is worth your time to be present and how much time you dedicate to each event. We will address this topic in more details in the chapter on Time Management.

6. Do not forget the values of *The Unique Lawyer System*

Before being a lawyer, remember that you are first a human being, determined, in society, by the values you share or do not share with your people. These values in which you chose to believe and then used to guide your actions will also cross over into your professional activities. One of the values in which we believe, for instance, is the need to contribute to saving the planet. We consider *The Unique Lawyer System* to be involved not only on a personal level, but also in a professional capacity in such initiatives.

Be human, do not forget the less fortunate. If you have worked hard to become a successful lawyer, we highly recommend you to not forget where you started. To try, on a personal, but also on a professional level, to engage in charitable causes. Consider that your presence and taking actions for various humanitarian causes is important. I have participated in many activities for humanitarian causes and, sadly, very few law firms were represented there.

That is when we realized we had to act somehow, to take over the new initiative! We attempted to create events that offered lawyers the opportunity to contribute to various humanitarian actions. We were surprised to find that there were many lawyers who make numerous humanitarian gestures but did not want recognition. Modesty is, of course, a virtue but sometimes it is advisable to let our actions inspire others. From this premise we created the ELawVation platform and the "Be Different" foundation where we create projects for lawyers who want to make a difference and in this respect: "Unique Lawyers".

It has been said, "If you want to become a successful lawyer, you have to start giving away your success." We each have something to give to others. So, all we have to do now is move on to the facts. These little gestures sometimes make you unique and different. In the end, everything is an investment and definitely the results will appear. The benefits are greater when you do not do too many calculations and you give naturally and joyfully, according to the heart's will.

7. Be organized and structured

We all know the quality certifications in the functional structure of a company. In a law office, we consider the dossiers, the organizational chart and a functioning program that ensures the efficiency and quality of the legal act to be fundamental necessities. For a lawyer, any document is holy. How many lawsuits have resulted in financial loss from carelessness, clutter, lack of organization and communication within the office?

We recommend that you improve the quality of your law office. This improvement not only eases your workload and improves efficiency but represents an added value and credibility for clients and potential clients. The people who stepped on our law office's doorstep to appeal to our specialized help have always had the opportunity to see that we understand how to structure our work and organize the files. It has always given them a sense of trust and security, as they have confessed to us, and we see that our work is appreciated. Over time, that has brought us more clients.

8. Create yourself as an intelligent person

Let's not confuse the image with the labels! It is well known that the visual impact transmits information to the subconscious level. A logo is important and defines you, especially when it comes to a law firm. The general public remembers the names of lawyers less than they do the logo of that office.

This is why we recommend that you give this issue priority and choose a logo that represents you. Establish your fields and sphere of action and contact a specialist to adapt them into a representative logo.

On the ELawVation platform (www.elawvation.com) you will find a product designed to help lawyers to better position themselves in the market through personal development.

9. Train yourself and your team

Choose your team, partners, and collaborators smartly. Your team is your calling card. Personal development training programs for your team are essential. In fact, the concept of personal development represents one of the basic values of the ELawVation platform.

Looking back, we can now say that the biggest problem throughout our career was probably team management. It took us a long time to understand what was not working. At first, we were not well aware of what it was all about, but when we discovered coaching internships, everything changed. Focusing on this aspect of personal development needs, we were motivated to take coaching courses, then to become coaches ourselves and launch the first international personal development project for lawyers.

10. Act sustainably

Along with image, brand and ISO are also very important to your professional operations. Show that you care about your environment by using recycling devices and recycled paper. If you have ever gotten a book made out of recycled material, you have probably noticed that it captured your attention in a totally unique way, starting from the tactile sensation when browsing through it, to the graphics and the smell of the ink. When we started using recycled paper in the office, we were told that it did not have a very appealing look, but I reminded those people that they could not deny that the look was definitely different. We are not talking about appearances; we are not urging you to make these little changes because it is so fashionable. We truly believe that these little gestures help you make the difference. As CSR Programs (Corporate Social Responsibility) in law offices begin to be used by many people, we will begin to see obvious results.

11. Be passionate

Your potential for enthusiasm is the reservoir from which you feed. In one of the following chapters we will address the concept of a healthy lifestyle and trying to adapt it to the profession of being a lawyer. We believe that passion is an energizing tool that cannot be bought. It is activated when you like what you do. Moreover, it can be contagious. Clients prefer to work with a passionate lawyer rather than with a sad and bored one.

How do you think you can inspire more trust? Expressing your passion, which is, the inner state that adds value to your uniqueness. Any lawyer who wants to make a difference must be passionate about his profession.

12. Your work environment represents you

The first impression you send to a client when he visits you is extremely important. Any visitor will have the opportunity to first admire your office. That is why we recommend that you do not neglect this space. Pay attention to details. Replace objects or furniture that are too classic and rigid and adopt a more sober but harmonious design. Combine colors and materials so you can create an atmosphere that represents you.

The Secrets of a Successful Lawyer

When we launched our first book, we were not at the beginning of the road; we did not build a theory that we were just going to put into practice. On the contrary, we planned to share our life experience – both personal and professional – which has led us to a turning point in our lives. We have chosen to value the uniqueness that we discovered after a long journey of looking for our authentic selves. We realized that each of us is different and by accepting this with joy and enthusiasm, we could change the world we live in.

Then I understood that the two of us, in our own way, could make a difference by choosing to speak to people – through books, our websites, through media appearances, and through the courses and seminars we organize. We would introduce a new concept, which we believe could change peoples' lives: the "Be Different" concept.

After we had sketched the main lines of this new action paradigm to obtain a new lifestyle in accordance with the uniqueness of each person, we intended to offer strategies that could be applied to different professional areas. For the successful professional, the "Be Different" concept means personal development beyond the theoretical training specific to each field, as well as responsibility. "Be Different" addresses to all those who want to create value through their actions; paying attention to the human factor and the implications it has in professional relationships.

By knowing themselves, appreciating inner strength, and by defining their own values, each professional can contribute to improving their personal life and making a positive impact on those with whom they interact. Self-knowledge brings with it the accumulation of recognized values; not only for yourself, but also for those whom you can relate with beyond the professional level.

In the previous chapter, we urged you, by means of some practical recommendations, to try to be unique in your profession. We believe that, in a constantly changing world, full of challenges, this is an indispensable quality of the successful professional. We strongly believe that a successful lawyer must be part of *The Unique Lawyer System*, a professional whose focus in his professional stature is to Create Excellence using both competence and self-knowledge and the skills to network with others, for the purposes of sympathy and empathy. This is why we suggest, in this chapter, some rules of conduct that will help you discover how you can assert your uniqueness in your legal career while obtaining and maintaining the prestige of a successful lawyer.

I. Be trustworthy!

First of all, strive to be the one that others can count on. Before any professional contact, establish a human-to-human connection and maintain it throughout the professional relationship. Many lawyers begin well, but very few manage to maintain this connection. Clients come to you because they are in a situation they cannot solve on their own. Most people are not looking for a law review. They do not need legislative debates, nor are they impressed by legal terms. Most people want you to solve a problem for them. Establishing a trust relationship is not only based on the first impression, but also on continuity. Stability is fundamental.

Find solutions, persevere, and improve yourself continuously! Do not abandon this principle until your conscience is reconciled. Be serious about solving the problem. Do not add other problems to the already existing problems of your clients. Stay in touch with your client. Inform them about what you are doing for them. Answer the phone or send them a message and do not miss deadlines. What our clients want is to find someone they can rely on to make their lives easier.

It is not enough to know the law, it is important to be useful to your clients. From our experience, we have noticed that there is a real difference between simply being a lawyer who knows the law and being, besides that, a professional concerned about knowing the person and being interested in human nature in general.

Be a person interested in the best interests of your client! It is very nice for a client to consider you more than just a lawyer, which means recognizing your professional value, but also your human quality. It is a very sensitive line between the human and the professional side of your personality. The art with which you harmonize in a balanced dichotomy can guarantee the communication relationship that the clients want from you. It is about how you are transmitting when you manage to communicate beyond appearances, to let go of the arrogance, the sober ice mask that we have taken on by virtue of a defined tradition of the profession.

We wondered, at some point, why there is such a sobering attitude from the lawyer in relation to his clients. As I was saying earlier, in our society, the legal profession does not enjoy the prestige that it deserves. This is perhaps because some lawyers have managed to discredit the image of the guild through abuse of their power. Whatever the reason for the diminished positive image of the lawyer in society, it is important that we all work to recognize the importance of the role of this profession. This aspect can give rise to mutual respect in the lawyer/client relationship and to bring the human touch to any relationship, both personal and professional.

We know that lawyers understand the law, but it is not enough if you want to become a Unique Lawyer. Try to broaden your areas of concern: read books, go to the movies, take part in social life, and go to debates. You will meet new people; you will be able to talk about things other people find interesting and thus you will be able to have erstwhile discussions with your clients.

Most often, your clients do not possess legal knowledge and therefore cannot assess how well you know the law, but you can instill confidence through other aspects of your personality or broaden your knowledge base. These little details, the little informal discussions, can convince the person in front of you that you are a curious person who studies, stays informed, and that you are most likely to seek the most appropriate solution for his problems.

II. Know your client better to gain his trust

We live in a transitional period, as we have said in the course of this book. We believe that we are in an era in which people should return to their human side and that the first step comes from within each of us. A lawyer, perhaps more than other professionals, should possess those skills of human knowledge that help him when working with people.

Working with people is the most beautiful, but also the most complicated task.

During our childhood, my sister and I enjoyed an education based on interpersonal relationships. We often remember the words of our father — *We are all God's children*. This was the starting point of our career when we reported to our first employer. We were always open, and we tried to see the man behind the legal problem that we had to solve. It was not a common attitude in the practice of law in our country. On the contrary, the typical attorney, can be recognized from afar: by their superior air and that sometimes arrogant attitude when communicating with his clients.

We also went through a period when we had a "God complex". It is a condition that surely many of you have experienced or applied to other colleagues. After observing some of them closely, sometimes this observation will prove to be completely unfounded. In another chapter, we discussed the self confidence that a lawyer must have. We still believe that it is good to keep a handle on this, because any quality can turn into a flaw. There is no one recipe that can be taken from books or orally. Our goal is to offer you a few guidelines, which will help you successfully design your career as a lawyer. You must adjust your "recipe" to fit your own personality profile. That is why we consider good self- knowledge to be an essential quality in both professional and personal life.

We have found, from our experience, that a professional attitude that inspires confidence and that gives the client a sense of safety and trust is not necessarily a given when it comes to the personality of a remarkable lawyer, but an asset that is built over time, with much work and experience. Your clients need to have a sense of safety founded on truth, not on delusions. Your client is appealing to your legal expertise because he has already facing problems. He does not need additional problems caused by the attitude of the lawyer. We believe that we must express great care and attention to detail in the way we treat our clients, because they are our mirrors.

III. Your motivation counts

Human actions and behaviors are triggered by various motivations.

Human actions and behaviors are triggered by various motivations.

Motivation is a process of energizing and stimulating the entire system of our being. It is the engine of movement. The term comes from the Latin word *mover*, meaning "*what pushes to action*".

Think about what led you to choose this profession. What is your vision of a successful lawyer? Do you think about prestige, success, money, and vacations or are you thinking of a responsible person that people need, depend on and can count on? Whatever your motivation is, it will support you in fulfilling your expectations for yourself and your clients.

Good self-knowledge implies an awareness of what motivates you in your career towards achieving the goals you have planned. That is why we think it is good to ask yourself right from the start what motivates you personally. During your career, having flawed motivations and goals can lead to various inner conflicts. If the emphasis is only on the material aspects and factors related to feeding your ego – pride, fame, reputation – you can risk pushing yourself away from your initial motivation. An inner conflict can also arise when you collaborate with partners who are not on the same level of communication as you. This can also happen when you accept files and clients without having the necessary resources to manage them, motivated by the prospect of financial gain. There are antagonistic situations that can generate uncertain moods. You will wake up and find that your enthusiasm has disappeared while you feel the lack of energy.

You cannot raise the claims of having clients of a certain level if you are not already at that level. Whatever the field you choose, the important factor is your determination, that energy that you will release. Choose to be successful, to be the best. It is not, however, a simple choice. You need to act and be organized. You will find more tips on this topic in the chapter that refers to Time Management.

We wanted so much to succeed at the beginning of our career! I was the passionate one. It was like I had radar that received all the radio waves that led to success. It was taking us to the right place at the right time. We always knew we would be successful.

Just like intellectual capacity and knowledge, desire is essential. It is the inner fire that makes you try harder to get what you want, to win, to search diligently for solutions to your clients' problems. The streets are full of intelligent and trained people who do not know how to efficiently channel their potential because they lack this inner impulse. It is desire that pushes you to act.

It is not enough just to think or have good ideas. The important thing is to harness the skill and determination to put them into practice. You will not suddenly have a fascinating career. No one has it from the beginning. The secret is simple: the great successes are the result of a sequence of ordinary days in which you do not give up on the firm decision that you have to do quality work and be the one that others can count on.

And, last but not least, do not forget this important fact. Do not let yourself be dominated by what people around you say. There is a lot of envy in the world. Do not generously share your desires, for you risk wasting them. Just be yourself and trust the divine source that supports you.

Unfortunately, there are many social beliefs, many preconceived ideas that attempt to deter us from traveling on our chosen road. But many times, these setbacks can even prove to be the source of our motivation. These beliefs exist and we must be aware of them, but we should not let them stop us from taking the right decisions.

We once had a client who had a very important name and a difficult case. He had been to a lot of lawyers who did not give him a chance of winning. He was disappointed and had no hope. He arrived in our office, but initially we did not want to give him hope, although we wanted to be able to do that. We knew he did not have much of a chance, but we accepted the case. Finally, we managed to help him earn more than he could have imagined because we believed we would succeed, and we were determined to seek solutions.

IV. Be enthusiastic and enjoy what you do, just like you did at the beginning of your career!

We know that experienced lawyers find it even harder to be enthusiastic, but we believe that notion is a bias; a culturally accepted viewpoint. Let us focus on what is important, which is to enjoy what we are and what we do.

We started on our professional path with enthusiasm, but along the way, we lost our joy. If the same thing has happened to you, you might want to try to remember the reasons why you should be happy in your career. In any situation there is a positive aspect, depending on your perspective. You can either look at yourself as an abused professional or you can express gratitude for what you are. The state of gratitude, the reconciliation with oneself will always generate enthusiasm.

Enthusiasm is directly related to motivation. The more established you get in your career, the harder it will be to keep a high level of motivation. It is important, therefore, to identify the source of your enthusiasm. Enthusiasm does not last when your motivation lies in the desire of earning money or in personal affirmation. We need genuine, healthy enthusiasm that comes from the call to be in the real service of others that is derived from the desire to really contribute to the quality of life of your clients. In doing so, you can easily manifest enthusiasm in your professional life, and people will feel attracted to your energy like a magnet. Clients will search for you and will feel safe around you.

You may not continually feel the enthusiasm as much as you did in the beginning of your career, but by addressing a wider perspective, including your personal and professional plan, your enthusiasm will continue to grow.

All that being said, if you still cannot find positive aspects in what you are doing, try being useful to the people around you and be happy that you can help them. Do not give up being a dreamer. Have the courage to feed on your dreams and unite them under the motto "People for people". Do what you do with passion. It is the purest source of enthusiasm. Keep the potential of unexhausted enthusiasm, try not to bind yourself to titles and functions, but remain curious and open to the new. Do not let yourself be conquered by money, but concentrate on what you are working on, on the subject of your cause. Get involved and be present.

Another source of enthusiasm is the belief that you are on the right track. We, for example, are guided by conceptualizing and popularizing the paradigm "be different" which helped us see things differently; to consider that any obstacle is just a different moment and not the end of the road. This helped us keep our inner flame burning brightly.

Think about yourself. What makes you happy? What do you need to achieve your goals? How can you contribute through your professional and personal resources to get abundant amounts of what brings you joy? Set goals and maintain your enthusiasm. How? Here is a suggestion: you can try to do something different besides your normal professional activities. Help young lawyers. Encourage them with care and passion. Get involved in other activities that can complement your professional life. Connect some of your hobbies to your profession. Choose a different approach.

You do not have to give up the career you chose. At the events we organized, I met many lawyers who wanted to quit the profession precisely because they could not rekindle the enthusiasm from their first years in practice. Change your perspective and you will have a renewed enjoyment of this profession.

V. Trust yourself

You are a very smart person, otherwise you would not be at this point in your life. And give yourself credit for the fact that you are interested in reading this personal development book. Clearly, you understand that, besides legal knowledge, you also need information. All this demonstrates that you are gifted with a certain dose of emotional intelligence, which is valuable and worthy of further development.

You have probably noticed a somewhat ironic fact: we often act efficiently, and behave intelligently, but we do not know how to place value on our own efforts. How important is this issue? It is enough to remember one thing that is easy to see: if you become aware of the value of your actions, if you gain confidence in your own abilities, you can overcome any limit. **Do not expect others to trust you if you do not completely trust and believe in yourself**.

The development of your career as a lawyer is a personal matter. Each of us is responsible for the road we take, for our own style and for the approach that characterizes us. The goal is to build a reliable relationship with our clients. But only a few of us understand that the most important relationship of trust that we have is to build the relationship with ourselves. We must take responsibility for the values we choose to believe in. Invest in yourself. Worst case scenario, you may lose business, but the investment in yourself remains. It is a constant. A person with stable self-esteem will never compare himself with others. Be unique! You are different. This is the subject of the book we wrote a few years ago titled "Unique and Different".

Build a different thought process. Put yourself in a positive light and get rid of limiting beliefs that come from others. Usually this silent takeover occurs within the family unit and in the environment in which we were raised. Parents attitudes are very important because they can influence the child's self-esteem. Access and review your childhood memories. Have you ever been told that you are good at something and that you can succeed? Or have you been told repeatedly that you will fail and that you will be a nobody?

Alina: *I have struggled a lot with distrusting my own strength. Although I had good results, I could not own them because, no matter what I did, I did not feel satisfaction and I did not perceive appreciation from people around me. Even though I was earning high grades at school, the response was, 'it is normal, but you can do better'. The word 'bravo' did not exist. It was a form of emotionally destructive motivation, and it affected my confidence in my own abilities. We have worked hard to build this trust.*

All these aspects are quickly reflected in one's professional life. An approach that is based on trust brings added value in the client-lawyer relationship. That is why we recommend you invest in yourself. Be brave and get the needed experience to build and establish trust in yourself. The more you trust yourself, the more your clients will credit you with a consistent capital of trust.

Identify your resources and strong suits that may be able to strengthen your reputation. Work on your weaknesses in order to increase your confidence in your own potential. People with high self-esteem are pleasant, serene, and easy to communicate with. They are focused on great goals and are willing to listen to others. They do not take things personally, do not get upset, and do not dwell on petty things. This is why they get results.

Self-improvement is unending. Most of the time, this fundamental factor of success is overlooked. Do not wait for someone to teach you how to trust yourself. Take the time to know yourself and remember that you are the most important person in your life. Positive affirmations can help a lot. To develop this attribute, we recommend the book "Positive Affirmations" written by the American author Louise Hay.

VI. Invest in yourself to adapt to the new requirements of the world you live in

If we refer to the current market, even for the most talented, there will always be competition. But the greatest competition is with us or, better said, with our expectations. We have noticed countless times how our clients or other businesspeople, have great difficulty in adapting to certain situations. It takes a lot of determination and ability to adapt in order to succeed. Some lawyers are comfortable, whether or not they have clients. They do not do anything differently, even if they see they are losing clients. We trust that you do not share this mindset. This is because you understand one essential thing: that having abilities besides legal related skills will direct you on the path of being a successful lawyer.

There is a *secret* that not all lawyers realize, but any successful lawyer puts into practice. It is very simple. Whoever you are, whatever your specialty is, whether you choose to dedicate yourself to an individual career or work in a law firm, you are responsible for your own success. Therefore, improve your skills, use all the resources you can access to succeed. It may take extra effort for success but it is worth it.

Being a lawyer means continuous dedication and aspiration to excellence. Society has very high expectations from lawyers, which feeds the tendency towards competitiveness. You are really competing primarily with yourself, but you do not have to sacrifice yourself in the process. Invest time in your development and do not stray from your values. Seek to establish a balance between personal and professional values.

VII. You alone are responsible for your professional success

Regardless of the people you are dealing with or the cases you have accepted, you must realize that you and only you are responsible for how things will evolve in your career. The way you represent your clients, and the way you prepare for each case or how you solve each issue all depends on you. If you take responsibility for what you do, you increase your chances of gaining more clients. The best advertising for us as lawyers – the only one that counts most of the time is the recommendation from a satisfied customer. It is significant to note that in our first eleven years in business, our office did not have a website, but we flourished most during that period of our career. New clients were coming to our office due to favorable recommendations. Today, an online presence is indispensable. Most clients will usually visit the lawyer's website long before coming into the office.

We are convinced that you will soon see beneficial changes, especially if you are willing to take full responsibility for:

- Your workload
- Your peer relationships
- Success in client portfolio development
- Your professional and personal development
- Relationships with your customers
- Your activity, total commitment, passion, and pro bono work
- Your professional reputation
- Personal involvement in the community
- Continuous search for the most appropriate strategy in professional activity

Take full responsibility for every aspect of your professional practice and you will make a difference. Be a Unique Lawyer!

VIII. Get involved in the community you belong to

Offer added value to your clients and you will be a successful practitioner! Add value by what you do in your community and you will create a business that will bring you fulfillment professionally as well as personally. Get involved in events that help people around you, for example; actively support organizations that work with single or abused women, assist students who may not understand their rights, participate in radio and TV shows, or write articles for various publications.

Be an active volunteer. Only then will you be noticed and be able to adapt to the needs of the society you live in. We strongly believe that the role of the lawyer, as a fundamental part of society, must be expanded. He must regain his prestige and the only way he can do this is by involving himself in the community.

But success has its responsibilities. Are you ready to take them on? Do you know what to do if you choose success? What changes are you willing to make? What investments of time, energy and money are you willing to make? What exactly would you give up?

IX. Efficiently use the time you have

We are usually reluctant when it comes to allocating time to establish effective objectives. This takes second place after solving our clients' problems. Often, the key to success is in the awareness of what you lack or the resources you have in order to find the right solution. The capital of time and energy that you dedicate to rushing to solve a problem can be more carefully managed. In addition, you can acquire new skills in this way, improve your resources, and achieve more goals immediately. *Hurry slowly* says an old Latin dictum.

Efficient use of time and strategic moves are vital to learning how to establish ourselves in our careers and achieve our goals.

X. Experiment with new things

Have you ever felt stuck in a professional role that is not in line with your personal values? Do the duties of your profession restrict your freedom and stifle your creativity? Well, maybe you are just the right person at the right time! The society we live in is a world in continuous motion and in perpetual reinvention. A career in the legal field is not exempt from the reality of this trend. Perhaps your mission may be to develop a new type of law firm; one that allows lawyers and team members the freedom to work on the cases they choose. A virtual office, for example.

Today the system is no longer the same. Classic law needs to break out of the old patterns. The Era of Technology forces us to act differently. The expectations have changed, which is why the approach must change. You can adapt or fight the system. It's easier to adapt, but you will be successful only by applying your personal style, thus helping to shape the system yourself.

XI. Give a positive sense to your inner voice

If you are convinced you are not going to be successful, then you can be sure that others will agree. Despite numerous achievements and numerous professional successes, do you continue to have doubts about your abilities? Why?

There is a negative inner voice that betrays you and offers a constant flow of negative ideas and feelings. Lack of self-esteem can lead you in this direction. Any positive results must be celebrated, and any loss must be seen as a brick in the construction of personal success. That way, you can eliminate those inner voices that block you when you are on the right track.

Another temptation that can take away your focus from your own path is comparing yourself to another colleague. This triggers the process of self-criticism. The fact that we are different does not mean we are less worthy than other people. Each of us has good moments and not so good moments in our lives. Therefore, we advise you to be gentle with yourself. Accept yourself as you are and persevere in what you do.

Andreea: *As a coach for lawyers, I met a significant number of legal specialists, who faced an over-active interior critic. This is a critical inner court that cannot be silenced, but you must know that there are effective strategies for transforming this negative inner voice into a positive one. We encourage you to continue working through the pages of this book to learn some new skills, and to further help build your self-confidence, you are invited to join the seminars we organize within the eLAWvation platform (www.elawvation.com).*

XII. Consolidate the feeling of personal value

Realizing that you have the decisive role in your career development, you can fully assume the responsibility of this role. This implies that you do the work of developing a solid foundation of self-confidence, because it will strengthen your feelings of personal value.

The development of your business is a personal matter. You can create it depending on your own style and approach. Broadly, however, we recommend that you focus especially on human relationships and trust. Your personal values are very important. Actually, those values are the basis of your attitude. When you have defined a system of values that you strive to follow with consistency, you know your personal boundaries and standards, and you will know which reference models to position yourself with. Thus, you will have shaped an inner environment to express yourself. It's like marking your territory. You may say there are limitations, but we believe in their necessity. In the context of cultivating the values you care about, these personal boundaries are able to impose a dignified attitude, which attracts the respect you deserve when marketing your service to a certain type of client.

XIII. Access a new professional level through specialized coaching

Andreea: *I cannot convey, through a simple description in the pages of this book, the meaningful coaching in a professional way. I think you can fully enjoy the benefits of it if you follow my exhortation and experience it for yourself. When I first discovered the tools I now share in my coaching sessions, I lamented the fact that I had wasted time and energy by not using all these techniques, approaches, and practices (you will find them in the "Unique Lawyer System" on the www.elawvation.com website) that improved the quality of my life, and the performance of the lawyers on our team, which has enriched our entire law practice considerably.*

XIV. Create order from the chaos

A typical method for lawyers is to work erratically, with many different matters and projects that inevitably will require different priorities. This practice leads to stress, panic, and insecurity. At some point, you will feel the need for a different strategy. This may mean that you find it necessary, first of all, to close the accounts that cannot comply with your new ways of doing business and set ting boundaries. If you manage to stop the chaos, you will automatically stop additional stress. Thus, your organizational and planning capacity is activated and will maintain a state of clarity that helps you achieve a state of normalcy as a successful lawyer. Allow yourself to be successful. Many times, the state of chaos sabotages you, not letting you advance to greater success. Ironically, the fear of success is one of the biggest roadblocks that prevents you from having it.

Taking power is not simple because it involves many responsibilities and waivers. Leaving your comfort zone is one of them. There are people who prefer to sacrifice success for comfort. Give up the chaos in your life and relax. Assume your success with dignity, because you deserve it.

It is said that a successful person tends to be calm. In a special chapter dedicated to stress we will focus on specific techniques to eliminate stress. Knowing when and how to say STOP is one of them.

XV. Know your weak and strong points

It is not easy to define yourself and act accordingly. But you have likely analyzed your strengths and weaknesses through observing your feelings and behaviors in various situations. Any person who admits to being vulnerable in certain areas opens a door to his own growth in many aspects of his being.

Andreea: *Experience has guided me to identify my strengths and taught me how to evaluate them so that I can find the path to success as easily as possible. The result was a remarkable increase in my efficiency and productivity. It gave me the confidence to believe that I have control over my career.*

One of my strengths was the fairness and quality of the services I offered. During my career, I realized I was a perfectionist. I could not promise anything without making that a priority for me. It is true, these strengths turned into a boomerang when I overreacted. Why do I say that? Because, being a passionate person, I demand a lot from myself, but also from those around me. Yes, it can also be called a professional defect. So, here is how a strong point can turn into a weak spot. It is important to be aware. One of my weak points was my lack of patience. I could not synchronize with the rhythm of people around me. Communication suffered and tension increased in relationships with my collaborators and clients. I could not bear to explain. It was all in my head. I was sure of what I was doing, and I did not consider it necessary to communicate.

In another chapter we talked about the importance of creating safety, credibility, and comfort for your clients. When you have more resources that you can offer, your effort diminishes, and the communication relationship improves. All these things I learned during my career, and the moment I started analyzing myself. When I started putting the spotlight on myself, things changed.

Every person is different, and it is their own responsibility to know themselves. We are talking about the knowledge of strengths and weaknesses, but also the awareness of the situation as a whole, to establish an effective strategy for one's career and life. In my MBA program, I studied SWOT[1] analysis (Strengths, Weaknesses, Opportunities and Threats). These are factors that support us when observing the necessity of restoring

1 The concept of the strategic SWOT analysis comes from a research conducted between the 1960s and the 1970s at the Stanford research Institute in the USA. The SWOT acronym comes

a situation, but also in making decisions. This model can also be applied in strategic decisions taken in our clients' cases. We will debate these topics more extensively in the Unique Lawyer courses.

Our qualities must be held in balance, as this is the key to success. If we use that key to lock and unlock, when necessary, certain parts of our personality so that we do not get stuck in an unproductive behavioral pattern, then we can say that we have the necessary craftsmanship in any field, but especially with ourselves.

The same goes for weak points. There are people who say, more or less directly, that they know it all or that they do not need to learn anything more. In truth, you do not get your whole life to really discover who you are. We all tend towards perfection, but a perfect person is the one who recognizes his or her imperfections. That is why it is important to ask yourself: how can I change anything if I am not aware of the need for change?

XVI. Learn to be a professional

We are not born with the ability to develop a business or with certain managerial competencies. We must strive to grow in this direction. It all begins with the inner strength of every lawyer and their motivation for success. Do you consider yourself professional?

If we start from what motivates you, then perhaps it will be easier for us to understand what this means to you. Broadly, we know that a professional is one who respects his commitments, one who pays special attention to detail and takes all due diligence to succeed.

There are some golden rules regarding a professional's thinking. Are you ready for this marathon? You have to know that the track on which you are running is called Integrity. Each successful person is guided by personal principles that meet in the integrity arena. To be successful you have to participate with everything you have. For us, integrity lies at the top of personal values, but each of us is different and has a personal standard.

When you want to reach a certain type of clients, when you want to work with prestigious corporations, understand that you need to obey

---

from English: Strengths, Weaknesses, Opportunities, and Threats. It is a method used in the business environment, to help design an overall vision of the company.

some demanding rules. Do not lose your integrity and your clients will respect you! There were situations where clients left us because they did not want to accept our principles, but after a while they came back and accepted them. We do not advise you to be rigid. There is no need for any façade of academic level and rigidity to promote your principles. Be relaxed and remain who you are.

Another component of this marathon is perseverance. A performance athlete trains on how to measure energy. We will address this in the chapter on Health. Establish a plan for your professional life, but also for your personal life. Use this book to learn techniques to bring balance into thinking, gain self-love, and maximize success.

When you set your goals, remember that the next step is to act in the direction of those techniques. Eventually, you will need a coach to check how you respect what you are learning. A good coach will remind you that the learning process does not stop once you have received your graduation diploma because life itself is a learning process. Socrates himself said,, "I know I know nothing."

Andreea: *I have experienced the attitude of lawyers who, when I talk about the Unique Lawyer, look at me with arrogance and say, "What am I going to learn?". I am not scared of this attitude, because I know it is about their defense mechanisms. People with this attitude changed after attending the "Lawyer Coaching" courses that we organized in 2011. Part of the motivation to write this book lies in the transformation I saw in my colleagues.*

Do not be shallow! A professional does not get high on false hope. He knows exactly where he is, and he knows that details matter. The level of auto analysis and activity evaluation is part of sanding the inner diamond. Therefore, let it shine on your best qualities in whatever you do, by deepening your engagement.

Stay focused on your objective. Once you have set your priorities, do not get distracted by everyday activities and temptations. Establish a personal ritual and stay focused on your goals. At the same time, learn to be flexible with yourself first. A self-demanding attitude will make you rigid and deplete your energy. Learn to conserve your energy and your time. Time is money. Set your goal to communicate elegantly with your clients. There is no need to communicate with them formally and rigidly. It's what distinguishes a Unique Lawyer.

When I embarked on this career path, I did not have this information and I did not know these techniques, so I had to learn them from experience. But you have the privilege of applying them on the basis of other people's experiences, the experience you will find in the pages of this book.

Alina: *I consider myself very lucky because I had pretentious clients and thus, I had the opportunity to develop a system of values in the spirit of competitiveness, first with myself. An inner voice guided me to the values that existed in me, but in a professional context I responded differently. I've learned that as a professional, quality matters and not quantity. Often, we hear what they say about some lawyers: "Ah... they have many clients." But ask yourself what is important to you: quality or quantity? Don't forget that every client is important in his own way and you can't afford to treat differently, because your success and professional standards would deviate from the level where you want to position yourself. Because how you position yourself is how you will be perceived. You can't afford to be lower your standards*

XVII. Don't forget to celebrate every success

With so much in your head, it is likely you wll forget to enjoy the little successes. Joy is the source from which your next success feeds. Learn to celebrate the successes you have achieved. Express yourself. Allow yourself to be a child when you are happy. As children, we did not receive words of appreciation for our successes. On the contrary, I was told that my achievements were normal or that they could be better. This can distort your representation of success.

Do not expect the people around you to commend you without first doing this for yourself. Offer yourself the gift of celebration for your own successes, and when you witness the successes of your colleagues, have the courage to recognize their success. Send greeting cards and words of appreciation. A lawyer is like an actor who gets applause at the end of the show. He lives to be acclaimed.

We must state that all the above considerations refer to the case of Unique Lawyer. In contrast, what can we observe today in our society? The fact that most lawyers are focused on the fees they collect rather than winning.

We believe that it is a sin to distort the image of the lawyer in society. This is the reason why we created the *Unique Lawyer System* (www.elawvation.com), which offers useful tools for forming a community of lawyers who know how to make a difference.

XVIII. Honor your law profession

In this section, we appeal to aspiring lawyers, with the hope that they will understand the responsibility they have towards themselves, towards their clients, and to the profession itself. This is a liberal profession that gives you access to a certain kind of public prestige, but it leaves you with very little time off. The beautiful part consists of diversity. We always deal with different matters and different people. A lot can be said about our profession, but no one could say that you have time to get bored.

But let's see how many can withstand a lawyer's typical schedule, full of changes and overloads. He starts his day with a coffee, around 8:00 in the morning and dives directly into reviewing files, which can last until after lunch. He is having lunch while running to meet a client who is waiting for him. Then there is a new meeting at a firm's headquarters. They meet for a few hours and then return to the office where they stay until late at night drafting documents, thinking about strategies and coming up with solutions for the clients and cases. Not to mention driving in traffic, attending public events, and handling family responsibilities and their social life.

As you can tell, the most important chapter in the life of a lawyer is the time management and personal organization. But we have approached a broader perspective, which indicates that everything is important: personal management, self-care, client care, time management, and any other tool that can help you achieve a balance between your personal and professional life so that you can enjoy this wonderful profession.

Andreea: *I'm writing in my office now. Its 7:45pm and I'm just wondering where I have found the energy after a day of work with three meetings and drafting some important responses. And yet I smile, I listen to my favorite music and I am glad I can bring a change in someone's life through these lines. I will write a little more and go to the gym where I will burn off the steam. At the end of the day, a massage at the spa relaxes me to help me detach all the negative energies accumulated during the day.*

Trust is not measured in units. Trust is a whole. A trusted lawyer is a competent person who has character traits beyond professional skills, has the power of decision making, distinction in action, and intelligent connections to the world. The opinion of a lawyer must be based on the rigor of a system.

CHAPTER 2

Get out of the patterns.

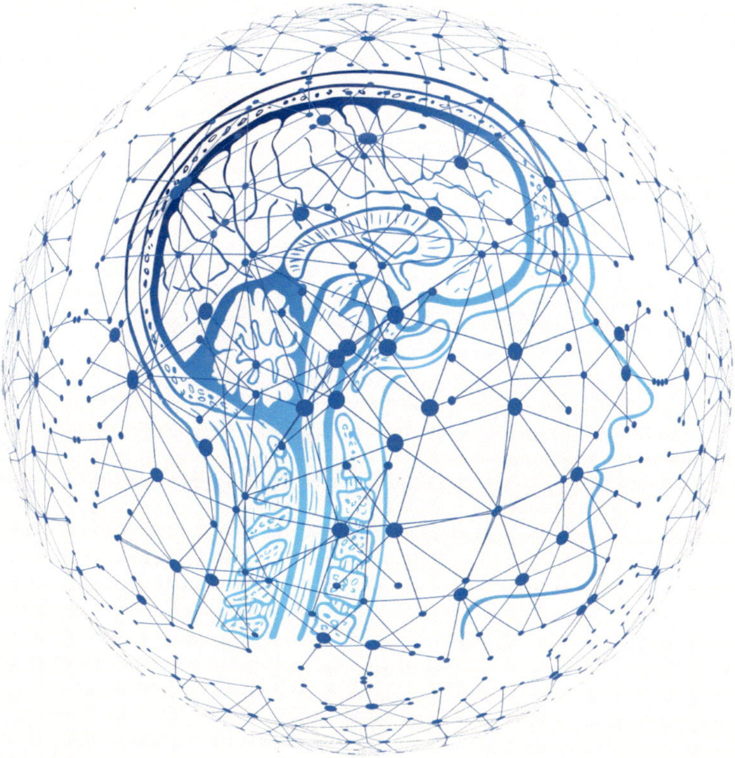

ONLY BY OVERCOMING YOUR LIMITS YOU CAN SHINE!

Chapter 2
Exit The Patterns!

The Image of the Lawyer in Society

There is a question of promoting a new image of the lawyer in contemporary society. It also emphasizes the need for professional training to continue in this field. Why is there a need for legal professionals to succeed in adapting to social changes? This is because old patterns no longer match the current requirements. Technology has changed our world, and clients' expectations are different. When we think of the position of the lawyer in today's society compared to the past, we find that we have to deal with two different images.

I know many lawyers agree with us, because we have had many discussions and attended many conferences where problems like this have not been resolved. In general, it is considered that other problems are more important. But if we think that the lawyer is the one who has to manage the rapport with his clients, the connection with the new society and social transformations, can we still avoid the alarm signal that calls us to change? Can we still ignore the need to be aware of the role of the lawyer, both in relation to self (to perform), and in relation to the exterior, to manage to cope with transformations and to identify the appropriate solutions?

How can you find a solution aligned with social requirements if your interior is not aligned with external transformations? The dialogue can be quite superficial if you think that a lawyer has precise lines to follow such as: law, jurisprudence, judge, and client needs, without considering the clients' personal needs. However, if this problem really concerns us, we will not propose a temporary solution. We will strive to produce some real and lasting changes. To achieve quality and stability, we must address professional activity without neglecting personal life in its intricacy.

Statistics show that stress is a phenomenon often encountered in the lives of lawyers. Stress makes its presence felt, more and more, right out of law school. A research study conducted at the prestigious Harvard University in the United States sounded an alarm some years ago — "Harvard Law School continues to represent, for many, both inside and outside the legal community, the high profile education... you would expect the faculty to be full of confident, enthusiastic, optimistic students who feel completely comfortable with themselves and who are fully prepared, after graduation, to face the world. Actually, you will find the opposite... [...] Even in the second year, a surprising number of students come to resemble what a teacher called 'wounded' — demoralized, discouraged and deeply uninvolved in the experience of law school, are worn down, withdrawn and insecure about their own value..."[1]

Psychological research on students shows increased incidents of anxiety. In the case of depression, the frequency increases by a percentage between 20 and 40 percent[2]. On the other hand, clients often rely on their attorneys with unrealistic expectations. This is when they are only rarely willing to contribute to solving their own problems.

From this perspective, we advise that an alteration in addressing the profession of a lawyer is needed. We are thinking of a review of the status and role of the lawyer in contemporary society that continues, naturally, with the development of a lawyer model adapted to the new social context. This new model — which we call the *Unique Lawyer System* — involves the application by any lawyer who wishes to adopt a different working

---

1 Making Docile Lawyers: An Essay on the Pacification of Law Students, in *Harvard. Law. Revue.*, 2027 (1998)

2 Kennon M. Sheldon, Lawrence S. Krieger: Does Legal Education have Undermining Effects on Law Students? Evaluating Changes in Motivation, Values, and Well-Being, în *Behavioral Sciences and the Law* 261–286 (2004), published online at Wiley InterScience (www.interscience.wiley.com)

model both with himself and with his collaborators and clients, so that his role in society will be accomplished with maximum efficiency.

The lawyer mediates between the law and the client, but the transparent wall between them can only be crossed through practical expertise, acquired by access to new and complex resources that facilitate the manifestation of an operational level different from the classic (obsolete and worn) methods.

The world is changing, and humans are adapting along with it. The role of the Lawyer is the same, which is to help others, but the new context obliges us to have a different approach. How can a lawyer become stuck in the classic lawyer model? We live in a time of many challenges, where attention must first be directed to the interior and then outward, without forgetting that balance is fundamental in this equation.

Each stage of history had its characteristics and certainly had individuals that marked the era through their deeds. There are, among them, lawyers who have linked their names to famous processes or outstanding achievements in the legal field, thus creating history when it comes to law and sometimes history in general. The history of great trials cannot be erased from the memory of lawyers. The question is whether we, today, contain such passion and dedication for the values of the legal profession.

There is a general impression that something in human consciousness has changed so much that the law has become like clay that can be shaped according to momentary interests. We do not want this to be a book of arguments or social satire. We want it to be a book to help lawyers find a clear direction in life, to help them put themselves first, not in a selfish, but a practical way. The principle underlying this approach is that you cannot give maximum efficiency to your neighbor if you do not invest in yourself first.

This book is based on the idea of empowering lawyers and giving them an awareness of the social role that they have. It is true that in many countries, respect for lawyers as individuals has decreased, which has also affected the prestige associated with this profession. However, we invite you to believe in the profession we have all chosen; in its beauty, in the spiritual adventure that it presents us, and in the people, who value the virtues of their profession. Alongside teachers, physicians, and priests, lawyers contribute to the circle of professionals who ensure the stability of a society.

As we have already pointed out, we believe that personal development responds to a fundamental need for self-knowledge and improvement of the contemporary man. Other people's lives depend on the quality with which each of us performs their professional role. As a psychologist has the obligation to enroll in a personal and professional development program, in the same way, the lawyer must take responsibility for increasing the quality of his services and to enroll in a program of continuous personal development.

This is how it was born the idea of the *eLAWvation platform* (www.elawvation.com), where you will find continuous development programs for lawyers. It is a useful tool for professional development and evaluation, in order to find balance and effectively manage the stress that a successful career can generate.

Andreea: *I now remember the momentum I dedicated myself to with one case or another, at the beginning of my professional career. Who do you think had priority for me; my client or myself? Of course, the client. I just forgot about myself and then wondered how I got to be affected by stress. In the crazy rush of every day, I never took time for myself, and I was not happy with my life. I know I am not an isolated case. On the contrary, in our profession this is rather the rule than the exception.*

In the following chapters we will analyze the typical problems of lawyers, but we believe that the most important and exciting thing will be the solutions. We hope that, after you have been through this book, your professional life, like your personal one, will be different. We want every lawyer to succeed and enjoy his vocation. We would like statistics on professional stress to fall, and respect for the legal profession to grow.

But all this cannot be accomplished unless each of us starts changing from within. When you respect yourself more, you love yourself more, and you are aware that you are the only one who acts in your own best interests – change happens. The change begins inside and, progressively, you will be able to observe it in the attitude of those around you.

People are used to waiting for external changes, which is why they trying to change people around them first. But it doesn't work that way. We remember the great lawyer, Mahatma Gandhi here, a symbol for the *Unique Lawyer System* we want to promote. He said, "Be the change you want to see in the world". The change begins with you, and from you it propagates to the world around you.

By the nature of his profession, the lawyer is a leader of opinion and a social leader in general. We can remember the great lawyers who contributed significantly to the change of the world alongside Mahatma Gandhi: Abraham Lincoln, Fidel Castro, Turgid Marshall, Samantha Power, Hillary Clinton, Tony Blair, etc. The above list can continue with Nelson Mandela, President Obama, Dimitri Medvedev, Nicolas Sarkozy, Christine Lagarde, etc.

Lawyer's label in society

One of the reasons for which we decided to write this book is that we want the image of the lawyer in society to be elevated. But this cannot be achieved without the help of our colleagues. On the other hand, this book is also dedicated to clients who want to make a good choice for solving their legal issues.

A successful lawyer – client relationship

They say the lawyer needs to know how to educate his clients. That is true, but it should be done with elegance and a steady spirit. We propose seven steps that we believe can help you in the process of educating your clients.

1. Know your value

For that you must, of course, be prepared. Be the master of the knowledge you need to get in order to help your clients. Do you know what your value is? You may have heard the expression: "Many would like to be a diamond, but few are left polished." When you know that you have invested in yourself, that you have been polished, you will not identify yourself with the labels placed on you or your profession. On the contrary, choose to shine unmistakably, inspiring inner trust. Remember who you are, how much you are worth, but do not be arrogant.

I have met so many lawyers who cultivate an arrogant attitude! It is an enormous mistake, which we have all made, but we realized that something was wrong, and we changed our attitude. Our motto is, "Do unto others as you would have them do unto you." So, we woke up and have continued to follow that wisdom. But there is a tendency that is easy to adopt when you know that the client's fate depends on you or you know you have the power. We will debate the subject of power in more depth in the following chapters.

Returning to personal value, it is good to be accountable to others, but also to the investment we have made in ourselves, in terms of time, study hours and, often, compromises. Why compromise?

Andreea: *I confess it has not been easy to manage some relationships with difficult clients, especially because I have an impulsive temperament when someone causes me to waste my time. For me, the hardest to face is the lack of logic, with the loss of time or with repeating the same discussion and unnecessary stories. It is about those clients who think that if they pay you, you have to be at their disposal and do not consider carefully your work schedule and your priorities.*

It is true that in some countries the image of the lawyer is extremely important in society, as a lawyer can be considered valuable just by their title. However, we consider that each professional must shine through their competences and the limits they establish related to client service. First you must be the one who establishes and protects your own values and then ask for that from others.

2. Do not let yourself be exploited by your clients

It is very easy to fall into this trap for many reasons. That's why we think it's preferable to define the objectives you're working on and make sure your client understands. Communicate certain hours and days when you are available for your case and do not deviate from this rule.

Alina: *The first example that comes to mind is that I was very passionate about what I was doing, and I was getting more involved than I was supposed to, and some clients were taking advantage of it. They were asking for one thing, and I ended up dealing with ten. My openness and dedication were taken as an opportunity to be given endless tasks, without them being part of the initial agreement. I was called late at night and even on vacations, I sat on the phone for hours, without setting boundaries. As I said above, we must set the boundaries. Another problem derived from here was that, when it came time to bill the hours worked, it required an extra negotiation of hours that were not predetermined. Besides the fact that I was feeling frustrated, I consumed a lot of energy recovering the fee they owed me for my work.*

3. Set your work rules from the beginning

Inform your client of your work style and your schedule. Of course, it is preferable not to be rigid. Everyone wants to be treated with understanding and respect. It is better to be open from the beginning and not to introduce new elements during collaboration, because the degree of trust will decrease. If from the beginning you communicate with tact what your schedule is, you will be respected and appreciated for sincerity and you will give proof of stability.

Negotiate the contract from the beginning and set your boundaries. It is preferable to explicitly present to your client that everything outside of the conditions set is part of another agreement. Communicate this agreement in a clear and concise way.

4. Delegate with tact

A big problem I encountered was that most of the clients wanted to talk to us personally about their matters, although there were other lawyers in the office who handled the files. Because we established the initial relationship, we were requested directly for all communications. It was impossible for us to be present everywhere. At one point, I was talking on two phones at the same time. It goes without saying that working in this way could go on forever. It would eventually prove to be ineffective to the client and downright destructive to the lawyer.

How can you cope with such a situation? Learn to present your team from the beginning as part of the project. Invite the people you work with and present them to the clients to help them establish the same sense of trust and safety with your clients that they have with you. Introduce those who you delegate work to by expressing your confidence in their competence and ensuring your client that everything is still controlled by you. When we learned this, we had a load lifted from our shoulders. I finally saw clients talking to other colleagues. It is all about habit. Of course, the delegation does not happen by itself. It requires repeated practice for the process to be successfully completed.

5. Request and provide written communications

We all know that there are times when you happen to think something and not communicate it, but you believe that you have communicated it, even though you only thought of it. Get your clients to send you all their requests in writing. This will also help you with billing, but more importantly, documenting everything helps to avoid any lack of communication that can lead to misinterpretations. You do not want to have to deal with reproaches when people assume you have not dealt with things that, in fact, have not been communicated to you.

6. Provide follow-up to all professional contacts

Although we were not taught explicitly, the habit of creating follow-ups seemed natural to us from the start. Regardless of the meeting we had in the business environment, we have always sent a few lines of what we discussed or at least a brief appreciation of the meeting. In doing so, we kept a channel open to future collaboration with that client.

Even if you set up a face-to-face meeting or a phone call, send an e-mail outlining what was discussed. I consider it an action that conveys respect for discussion that took place and who you spoke with. I also noticed that many prestigious companies use this model. Another advantage is that, by doing so, you can remember the context more easily and you can use notes and contact details for the future.

7. Leave no room for conjecture

In relation to colleagues, but also with our clients, we have always been exposed to unfounded discussion assumptions. How many times have I heard the words: "but I thought..." or "so I thought..."? Here is one aspect that we have learned to manage: to ask the right questions and to establish all the details from the beginning.

8. Do not present the sandcastle

Do not give the clients a chance just to pay you a fee. Make sure you understand their expectations, evaluate what you can offer and communicate clearly. Through our code of ethics, we know that we cannot take cases for which we do not have the necessary competence. Many times, the clients are unclear and expect a magic wand to solve their problems without thinking about whether it is possible or not. Many times, we find that we have to repeat the same things over and over again, explaining the law to our clients so they can understand it, however, it is an upsetting sensation to feel like we are speaking to closed ears.

The people we spoke with had the same questions or the same suppositions: "But it can't be so..." or "why so...", or "how is it possible to...?" Well, these clients are not an exception. On the contrary, we often deal with people who have not studied law and have no connection with the legislation in force. Therefore, we consider it good to be, from the beginning, as explicit and concise as possible. Leave no room for assumptions, use written communications when dealing with legal issues.

The lawyers themselves are the first to admit that they are responsible for the way they are perceived in society. Jokes on their behalf represent attitudes we should get rid of. We must all work together to get rid of the arrogant attitude and the reputation that lawyers think *I am God* or *Without Me he is dead*! On the other hand, many of our clients have unrealistic expectations, but with tact we can establish a pleasant and efficient professional narrative that changes the rigid, lasting and imposing image, typical of the lawyer-client relationship, with a more open and humane one.

The Contract of Your Life

We were talking, in the previous pages, about the obligation that each of us has on our own, and about the promise we make ourselves. That promise is the most honest and most efficient one. It has the ability to increase your self-esteem, but it also gives you the power to overcome the obstacles you meet.

We see it as a gentle, atypical obligation, without thinking about sanctions in case we do not act at some point. It is not an obligation to third parties, but to us. This means something entirely different. It is a subtle promise that we are accessing in our being. We plant it and it grows with our help through our actions. Sanction, in this case, can only be a lack of joy. And joy is different when it springs from an inner motivation, from an agreement with us.

> Andreea: *As I said before, in my career I was motivated to have more success to prove to others that I could accomplish something, and that is because this is how our parents knew to motivate us. But when I learned how to access my inner values, my uniqueness, I understood that there was no need to prove anything to anyone. And that is the motivation I find primarily in myself.*

Because we are talking about a contract with yourself, we think it is good to define your contractual terms. Keep in mind that you have to set a timeframe in this contract. Although, in fact, the duration of the contract with us is unlimited, you will have to stipulate, however, several deadlines. Establish your objective, but also the term you intend to set.

Organization and discipline are two elements without which it will be very difficult for you to get results within a preset time. First you have to stay organized, clarify your strategy, then you will need to respect it. Maybe you are not used to abiding by such a contract. If you try to think differently, you will be surprised to see that it works.

Make a list of commitments to yourself and do not forget your rights. Count, among them the right to give yourself a reward, which you can enjoy when you obtain the desired result. Do not forget to celebrate the results you obtained. Do not neglect the right to relax with a well-deserved rest.

> Alina: *I remember starting, at some point, to act mechanically, just like a robot. I forgot I existed. The contract with myself was obsolete, and there was no way to attack. In fact, all I had to do was attack the rhythm that caught me up in those unhealthy habits that alienated me, removed me from myself. I was convinced that if you*

wanted to become a successful lawyer, you'd have to put yourself in the second place, become, basically, a workaholic. Those were damaging beliefs that I had in my unconscious mind which were misguiding me. Behold, in the end, I have come to be successful, but today I understand that you can reach your goals, in an equally dignified and perhaps more rewarding way, because they are duplicated by the satisfaction of the soul, and you honor your personal life.

We believe that, essentially, this contract with ourselves can prove even more beneficial as it seeks to respond satisfactorily to fundamental human needs that, systematically ignored, would cause dysfunction in the personality and the person's being in general. Researchers have shown that human needs, values, motivation, and relationships play a very important role in understanding the feelings of fulfillment and personal satisfaction. Psychological needs are fundamental to a positive life experience.

The unsatisfactory response to these needs' causes suffering, depressive tendencies, and loss of vitality. These universal psychological needs would be, according to the same researchers, the following: self-esteem, responsibility to others, authenticity, competence and sense of safety.

For those familiar with the pyramid of Abraham Maslow, these concepts are not a novelty. They are an additional confirmation of their importance. It seems that depression and emotional distress, with the incident raised among law students, would find their cause in ignoring these fundamental needs.

We believe that this type of dysfunction at the level of the individual's personality does not tend to disappear with graduation from law school and that many lawyers perpetuate them after entering this field. We hope that this book can help many lawyers manage their life differently and enjoy this wonderful profession. All you have to do is dare to see things from another perspective. Think differently to get different results.

Create a Great Vision

Our thoughts shape our future. So, do not limit your imagination in the work of building your professional future. Do not forget to consider your soul as an important variable in your ideal future plan. Do not lose yourself on the altar of success. In fact, it is not even real success, it is just an illusion of it. You should ask yourself, therefore, if it is worth sacrificing yourself for something illusory. So, keep the balance between your professional and your personal life, between the need to be successful in your chosen career and to feed your soul.

We think this commitment to yourself might appear as follows:

I commit myself to be the best version of myself, to develop professionally, to learn and improve continuously, to grow personally, to follow my dreams and to listen to my heart every day. I value relationships with people around me, showing respect and dignity to every person I come into contact with. Any relationship is an experience that helps me develop. I pledge to myself to give the best of myself and help others within the limits in which I have a role in the agreement established with them. I agree to enjoy my success, to be aware of my value, and to be satisfied with what I am and what I do.

Professional vision can sound like this:

Surpassing boundaries, I am a continuous source of creativity and I find solutions with ease. I am motivated by my success and the life I dream of; to study, to be curious and to continue to develop personally and professionally. My objective is to attract clients and situations that inspire me to grow professionally. My vision sustains me, encourages me and honors my dreams.

Create Your Inner Dialogue to Lead You to Success!

Words symbolize our mental experience, but social beliefs can influence us. Our brain takes words and turns them into visual representations, which in turn creates other receptors which together, generate other linguistic and behavioral schemes. Learn to act like you're already successful. Do not allow yourself to be arrogant, but you will find how beneficial it is to let the feeling of success invade you. It is a state that motivates you to employ the entire personal arsenal responsible for success: study, discipline, perseverance, optimism, faith...

Alina: *I remember, at the beginning of my career, I heard a saying that a good lawyer had to have at least ten years of experience. I ignored the voices saying, "You're not going to make it.", "You can't handle it if you don't have relationships.", "No one will help you" and other negative messages that we hear quite often from people who subscribe to some very resilient clichés in our society. Moreover, such messages were considered a motivation strategy that our parents also applied. I am probably not the only one who heard warnings like this: "If you don't learn, you'll be a nobody." But perhaps these voices from past generations have not had the resources that we have at our disposal today. Perhaps I myself, if at the beginning of my career would have benefitted from a book titled "More Than a Lawyer", definitely the energy capital used to fight these beliefs would have been invested in a more profitable way and it would have been easier to manage bombardments with negative messages coming from outside.*

Here are some helpful tips, which we have applied in our daily that can be of use: Make a list of motivational phrases and post them in plain sight in the office.

Make a personal commitment: that nothing will stand in the way of your success and that any obstacle can easily be overcome by adding a brick to the structure of your personality.

- You can start with phrases like:
- I remain focused on...
- My career vision is...
- I am inspired by...
- The best life I live is...
- I will manage my emotions every day...

You are the Mediator between Your Heart and Your Mind

Until now you have fulfilled your obligation to the profession and to the people you work for, but you have to learn not to neglect yourself and to make sure to educate your heart. A good mediator is one who can easily communicate with both sides. No one teaches you, during your professional training, how important it is to take care of yourself.

As I was saying earlier, we were the first to bring to the world of domestic law the idea of self-care, and we emphasized the importance of investing in ourselves. In this respect, we were the first voices to advocate for personal development programs for lawyers. We considered the fundamental and indispensable need to invest in personal development in order to serve others.

There is a difference between being successful and having success. You can be shot down by your own success when you think you own it. Being successful is nothing but continuous growth and authentically living in the spirit of joy and professional satisfaction.

Do not forget to let your heart be your guide; it is really the main advisor, that hidden mentor who can tell you what you have to do in certain situations. It has been shown that the electromagnetic waves of the heart are a hundred times stronger than those of the mind. It takes this balance between mind and heart to understand the rhythm you need when acting in your profession.

First you check on yourself, check your energy potential, but the heart is also your strongest energy source. You need a lot of energy to be able to give it to others. Learn to listen to your heart's echo and you will be surprised by the messages you will receive. You need quiet and calmness in order to let your intuition guide you and tell you the words you need to hear. In our profession, intuition is especially important when dealing with people who don't tell us the whole truth. Many times, intuition helped us ask the right questions to get where we were supposed to be when we were looking for a solution for our clients.

By employing both the heart and the mind in the process of searching for the truth, you will only be able to enjoy the clarity you will discover. There are little secrets that can help you manage this relationship between your heart and your mind. Meditation can help you enjoy a few minutes for your mind to rest.

In the *Unique Lawyer System*, we have several tools that help lawyers in this regard. In fact, this is our objective: to help as many lawyers as possible to maximize their success, while enjoying the achievements both in their professional and personal life.

Attitude towards Work and Professional Satisfaction

A positive attitude creates a positive working atmosphere. Joy should not be something random, it is the attitude you need to work efficiently and evolve continuously.

Create a pleasant atmosphere for others.

Surprise your colleagues with treats without a specific reason. There doesn't always have to be a reason to celebrate.

Think of pleasant ways to interact with your team or department.

Turn your office into a place where you enjoy spending time. Decorate your walls with photos, posters or poems.

Make jokes and maintain a positive attitude in the office.

Appreciate your colleagues for their efforts and recognize their merits.

Do not let yourself be discouraged by the inabilities of others and continue to believe in yourself and in your inner strength.

Always do the right thing, even if others don't.

Avoid participating in actions that can compromise your integrity.

Always be loyal to yourself.

Be proud of your achievements and reward yourself for what you did right.

Appreciate others for their achievements: friends, family, colleagues and acquaintances.

Resolve to become the type of person who recognizes good in others and values positive contributions.

1. Your attitude towards work

In most western countries, there is a certain kind of work ethic. The fact that we live in a society that particularly values entertainment and the idea of fun in general creates a rather ironic relationship between the individual and his profession.

After making considerable efforts to pursue training in a certain field and invest hopes and ideals in the process of obtaining qualifications and a job, a considerable part of our lives is filled with fear and even with the anguish of professional routine, looking forward to the weekend and the holidays.

The morning radio broadcasts begin on Monday with the countdown of the days remaining until Saturday. Wednesday is the middle of the week, and Friday morning means that the weekend has almost started. That creates what the psychologists call "Monday Morning Syndrome."

No wonder, statistically speaking, most heart attacks occur on Monday mornings. It is ridiculous how most people see their work as a necessary evil to pay the bills or as a relatively tolerable period of suffering for five days – the price paid in order to be able to relax for another two days. We live in a society of diseases induced by ignorance and inadequacy.

Dare to be different and create your own attitude.

Dare to be enthusiastic when it comes to your profession and your life!

Do not take part in the "I must resist" attitude but instead, join the attitude "I feel good". When people ask us what we're doing, we answer them: "Getting better every day", "Fantastic", "I'm fine."

Dare to be different from the others. There will always be people who feel the need to complain or who are afraid to stand out. Most people are used to not making changes for those around them. They are stuck in their current situation and are afraid to follow their hearts.

Do not deprive yourself of your little personal satisfactions.

Each of us have our own joys in life. For example, if baking a cake or eating ice cream makes you happy, stop thinking about the extra pounds every time. Feel good, take your time to satisfy, in moderation, your cravings. Or maybe meeting with friends, that unique moment spent with loved ones is one way to relax, even if you are tired and you have had a hard day. If playing sports or watching them manages to free you from tensions accumulated throughout the day, create your schedule so that at the end of the day, you have time for yourself to walk or jog. On the other hand, others are exactly the opposite. They find that physical exercise at night is too stimulating so they exercise in the morning and dedicate evenings for more spiritual pursuits.

Andreea: I have my morning and evening ritual. I start the day with physical exercise, running in the park or exercising after which I meditate, shower in the morning and thus I am prepared for a new day. I am a morning person. I like to wake up in the morning and dedicate at least an hour-if not two to three for myself. In the evening I like to relax, to do things that separate my mind from everyday problems, to read something that nourishes my soul.
A good physical workout and my personal development represent essential priorities for me in life. Today, before any professional obligation, my state of wellbeing is the foundation for a balanced life and for my professional success. If we do not practice wellness ourselves, we cannot offer our assistance to those around us.

In discussions with clients or with our friends we launched a small research study on our own, which provided us with a series of interesting answers. Among the answers was the preference for collaboration with lawyers who, besides professionalism and legal training, have taken a few steps towards personal development.

Such a professional would be more credible in the eyes of his clients if he takes care of his own health – body and mind. The long-term benefits of a healthy life extend to those around you – clients, employees, and collaborators. When you are healthy, you implicitly transmit it to those around you and you become a role model. Imagine what it is like to be in front of a lawyer who, after you present your problem, remains apathetic, because they do not have the strength and concentration needed to pay 100% attention to what you are saying. Important details can escape the lawyer's attention, especially if he is trying his best to ignore physical pain he might be experiencing during a meeting.

Law is a profession that requires one to practice good health, balance and vitality because each lawyer has a lot of responsibilities to their clients. If you want to fully enjoy the benefits of this profession, it is good to practice it in a state of harmony and balance, without stress.

We propose, therefore, a small exercise designed to give you a more faithful picture of your degree of satisfaction with the profession you have chosen.

2. **Professional Satisfaction Test**

Read the following statements out loud and observe what you feel when you read them:

- I am a successful lawyer.
- I am happy while practicing law.
- The profession of lawyer is my vocation.
- Every time I am in front of a customer, I feel confident about myself, I focus on the customer's problem and I want to find the best solution for him.
- The profession of lawyer gives me energy, freedom of movement and as the lifestyle I enjoy.
- The profession of lawyer gives me energy and I feel balanced, full of vitality and energy while working.
- Customer issues do not influence my personal life and I have the ability to separate my professional life from my personal life.
- My wellbeing cannot be negatively affected by my clients.
- By practicing law, I have enough time to rest, I have time for my personal life.

How did these phrases make you feel? Did you have a feeling of comfort while reading them or did you feel uncomfortable? How many of the above statements are true in your case?

Although you may be having a good professional period in which you feel that the roads are open to you, you are developing professionally and feel that you can move mountains, but from a personal standpoint, all things are not the same. At home, the atmosphere may not be congenial and your relationship with your life partner may be tense and you feel that your life is unbalanced. What are you doing in this situation?

Here are some suggestions that might help you find a solution:

- Try to keep a healthy balance between your professional and personal life.
- Avoid professional hazards and personal weaknesses.
- Change your unproductive habits, make positive improvements.

3. New habits in 4 steps

Easy to say, hard to practice! It's hard to change habits even if you have noticed they are harmful, and especially if you aim to achieve this fast. Here is why we suggest you make changes quickly; to adapt to new habits that are healthier, more productive, and in accordance with your own being.

First Step – Personal priorities

We remind you that at any stage of our life, it is good to set priorities. Ask yourself what the most important aspects of your life are.

Examples may include:

- Health: Sports, healthy food, vitality, energy.
- Family: Life partner, children, parents, brothers, sisters, etc.
- Profession: Study, professional development, professional activities, etc.
- Other: Hobbies, friends, networking, etc.

Second Step – Detecting harmful habits

Before engaging in various professional activities, even if it may seem very difficult or even impossible, commit yourself to managing your personal interests. Here we refer to those activities that you do outside of work hours. Try to reduce those behaviors that make you act like a robot — ready at any time to serve others and solve any problem.

Make this decision to change certain behaviors that compromise your best self, in order to correct the balance between your personal and professional life. In the long run, you will gain many benefits that you now cannot even imagine.

Third Step – Act!

Build yourself a personal start-up ritual. Choose two or three daily activities that are important to you and that make you feel like you have devoted time to taking good care of yourself. It does not necessarily have to be activities that take a long time. It can also be approaching an activity differently that you were doing automatically yesterday or looking at it from a new perspective.

Suppose you change the way you eat your breakfast. If you were used to eating it quickly, while reading the latest news or checking your email and your latest posts on Facebook, try changing this up a little bit. Realize that this is the starting point of your day and that you will be dedicating most of your workday to others. Start your day by devoting, above all else, a part of it for yourself. Have breakfast quietly and exercise for at least 30 minutes.

Exercising in the morning gives you energy for the whole day. Try to do something different from your usual routine. Start with a few simple things. Try a different approach and you will notice that your self-esteem will increase, and you will gain more confidence in yourself. You can apply the same methods to overcome other harmful behaviors.

Careful, though! If you try to change too much in a very short time, you risk stressing your body and causing a mental overload, even if there are significant benefits. Things must be changed a little at a time. Do not over celebrate every time you make a small change, because you may no longer feel challenged.

Again, the most important thing is to create a balance between your personal and professional life.

Fourth Step: Plan!

Here are a few specific steps that we think will help to lead you gradually towards this change. Start by creating a balance between the different parts of your life over a period of two to four weeks. When you notice that a certain segment of your daily routine is not getting enough attention, and that segment is important to you, you will have to start making changes in another part of your plan. For example, sports and exercise in general may be very important to certain individuals, however most people do not practice as much as they should.

Andreea: *I remember, in my first years of practicing law, my life was very disorganized: I did not even have time to eat, I even ignored the feeling of thirst when I woke up and I was still at the office until late at night. At the end of the day, I found that I was not taking care of the bare necessities. There was a time when I worked very hard, I dedicated most of my time to meeting clients and office work.*

What we propose through this guide and through the personal development programs we organize for lawyers is to create a different life agenda, whereby legal professionals will be able to achieve a state of equilibrium between their personal life and the professional one.

Postponing

We have spoken extensively about the degree of professional satisfaction and the little changes we can make in our lives to increase it. There are, however, a number of factors that may undermine this satisfaction from the very beginning. Postponement is among these factors. This is a sign of self-sabotage and is one of the aspects you should learn to control. Postponement can be caused by lack of self-confidence and stress. It keeps you from enjoying your job. The temptation of procrastination is one of the most important things you must work on if you want to develop a healthy attitude towards your profession. This noxious habit is worth trying to change to fully enjoy your professional career.

Often, procrastination finds its motivation in the desire to make things as good or as perfect as possible. This can be a huge obstacle in achieving your goals. When you notice that you are postponing something specific, make this your priority and complete it immediately. Perfection does not exist. Today's news will be old tomorrow. It's much better to confront important tasks in the morning when you're full of energy. Try to handle the issues you usually tend to postpone as long as possible in the early hours of the day.

Observe your clients!

The lack of satisfaction at our workplace can come, to a large extent, from flawed relationships with others, whether it be peers or clients. There is a theory in psychology, formulated by C.G. Jung that says our dark side, our shadow is built from everything we repress, what we refuse or deny in ourselves: "In our shadow lies the greatest treasure." This is a very interesting phenomenon. Anything we cannot see in ourselves or that we repress, we observe amplified in those around us.

The act of observing others is far from neutral. First of all, we notice what irritates us most in relation to it. But irritation is always born out of unconscious recognition. It is one of the most difficult things to accept: that the person who irritates you most reveals a part of you that you have never taken the time to acknowledge. Carefully observe what kind of clients, partners, colleagues or employees you get irritated with and in what situations and what kind of characteristics annoy you about them. Through a sincere analysis, you will find that the issues which are the most insufferable in the personality of others are those that are found in you.

I will give you an example. There are those who feel irritated by authoritarian people. What happens is that they are in denial of their own authoritarian attitudes in certain situations. Let us think, for instance, about the relationship with judges, in a professional context. An authoritarian lawyer will respond with an attitude of irritation, of anger in many cases. If this irritates you, it may be because there is a similar side to your own personality that you are uncomfortable expressing. At first this might be hard to accept, but knowledge is a first step towards self-awareness and for accepting those parts of yourself that you have so far denied that makes you complete.

You will know that you have accepted your shadow or your dark side the moment the people around you no longer irritate you. You can start this process immediately, because the most important part is to acknowledge it. You can share those attitudes, behaviors, and manners that irritate you with the people you work with in order to manage your relationships more easily. You should not try to change them but get to know yourself better and to work on your own issues.

Perhaps more important than the phenomenon itself is your desire to consider its existence, to be able to develop yourself in a personal way. Here is one of the main aspects that we refer to when we talk about *The Unique Lawyer System*: it is not a standard profile, which we can offer you ready-tailored, but a tendency that we invite you to discover in yourself, a boost that makes you seek to develop all the latent potential that lies in your being.

The Unique Lawyer System is, for us, a legal professional who cultivates within themselves a holistic perspective, but also on the relationship with clients, with authority, with everything that can contribute and can be considered, so that solving a matter will benefit both the client and him or her personally.

Your personal growth is obvious when other people no longer annoy you. Being able to see reality and from this perspective puts an end to the emotional blockage that some people still provoke. Even if, at first, you may find it difficult to accept the explanation of the above phenomenon, try to take our word for it. It is one of the most effective methods that can help you in managing emotions caused by these kinds of human relationships.

Another challenge that many lawyers face is the relationship with the opposing party. Here we recommend an approach meant to bring value to these interactions. Regardless of the attitude of the other party, the most we had to gain was when we maintained a respectful tone and tried to establish a civilized dialogue. People who are always unfriendly have a problem. Their dark side shows its fangs. As you project your shadow on others, they also do the same thing to you.

When you realize that, you will not take things so personally. It will be much easier to remain friendly and respectful with unfriendly people when you understand this process. You can understand the humanity of others and you can accept it exactly as it is. Their behavior cannot hurt you anymore, and they cannot influence your mood anymore.

That means being centered in your own power, so when you're criticized, you can accept it as a personal opinion of that person and not a universal truth. Acquire all that is useful from these circumstances and stay focused on your goal, which is solving the client's problem.

If you have the necessary time, perhaps you can read this chapter again. We believe that we can achieve love in this world, despite the misery and suffering we see around us. Work on the matters of your clients with love and you will notice different results.

Most human suffering is caused by ignorance and lack of understanding, so make understanding the basis of any relationship with your clients. Think about how nice it would be for those around you to do the same thing! It is not impossible. We are able to create a different world together.

Appeal to Your Conscience. Harness Your Strengths!

Perhaps you have often felt stressed by a client, a colleague or a collaborator. Well, you should know that there is a moment, a fraction of a second where you can choose to let yourself be influenced or even attacked by their remarks and enter into a negative state. Or you can choose to reject negative energy and focus on your own goal, so that you can easily get over a difficult situation.

As in any other profession, the attorney can meet with all kinds of cruel people every day. There are situations where we simply depend on another person to carry out the mandate. It is a situation where you have the choice: you will use replicas to change the behavior of others or focus on the objective pursued.

Andreea: *It happened to me many times, at the beginning of my career, when I went to different institutions to solve various problems for my clients, to be put in the situation of choosing to enter into a conflict or to move on, letting go of my vanity and solving the problem.*

The profession of attorney is one of those vocations where our ego can grow very large very quickly. Why do I say that? Because when the client appeals to the lawyer psychologically, he accepts that the lawyer is the one who can solve a problem, and his particular lawyer feels important to the client at the time.

Like any other situation in life, we can choose how we handle it. We can choose to go on the right and bright road of our own consciousness respecting ourselves or we can choose to go down the path of compromise and remove respect from our own soul. The moment you become aware that every thought and every action today builds your reputation tomorrow, you become much more careful about how you decide to manage every situation that puts you to the test.

This can bring you many advantages. First of all, it is a personal benefit, given the fact that you will feel at peace with your conscience when you choose to be fair, to be conscientious in what you do and to feel that you have made all efforts to solve a problem. Secondly, you will gain extra self-esteem the moment you know you've done all you can do.

People are human and will not act or will not always respond according to your expectations. In any case, if you are conscious of the thought that you acted in the best way possible, you must find a way to communicate this to your client or partners. I have often met special lawyers who did their job very well but did not know how to best promote their own value.

You Alone Are Responsible for Your Own Success

The *Unique Lawyer System*'s path is not easy. Throughout our career, we have faced a lot of complicated matters because we wanted to accumulate experience and we decided to be good at what we do. We raced into the ocean and started swimming.

We choose deliberately. When we chose not to settle for less professionally, we knew it would not be easy, but I knew we would make it. At the same time, we were prepared to accept the losses. There were ups and downs, like any road. We have convinced ourselves, in the process, that what is ultimately important is the state with which we welcome what life offers us.

Self-trust

Public speaking causes most of us a lot of fear. It was found that the fear of speaking in public is second only to fear of death. As a lawyer, you are probably used to talking before a judge but when you speak before an audience, it's different. In the chapter on communication you will find several techniques that will help you in the practice of public dialogue, both in front of a general audience and a judge.

There are techniques that help you discover your path to success. We believe that, in essence, this path involves managing the self. Each appearance has its own challenges, attempts, and obstacles. It is up to you if you choose to get out of your comfort zone.

A Unique Lawyer is the one who knows he can fly higher than he was told he could. Stay anchored in your dreams but be careful how you build them. First you must free yourself from the negative beliefs taken from the environment in which you live or even emitted by your inner voice, which can sabotage you.

In fact, self-confidence is something we build in ourselves but for that, we have to invest in ourselves. You notice that when you study and make some sacrifices, you don't necessarily go through pleasant times, because you are out of your comfort zone. But after you achieve results, you add stability to your self-confidence.

Perhaps you have made considerable efforts, and yet you feel that something is missing or that there is something that is blocking your progress and you don't know what that is. It is exactly those upsetting areas, the voices of those around you who stop you from your journey to success. Free yourself and rise above them. Imagine you are on a cloud that travels where you want to be.

Stay anchored in your dreams and notice how the effort diminishes. It is very important to know what you want, to have clearly established objectives and to consider all the necessary resources. It's like when you want to make a cake. You must have all the ingredients, because otherwise you don't get the taste you expect. For this it is necessary to have courage. Courage belongs to successful people.

Andreea: *I remember Anthony Robbins' seminars. His Motivational Motto was, "If you can't, then you must." You have to fight for yourself. It's an obligation you respect. It's your contract with yourself.*

Perseverance

Perseverance shows up in the decisions we make every day as we continue to try not to give up. Perseverance focuses on situations, feelings, and challenges that an individual face. When we feel lost, overwhelmed, betrayed or exhausted, we must know that we have the opportunity to choose a different way of thinking. If we accept the idea of delayed satisfaction, then we experience the joy of working for something difficult, knowing that it's worth it and that we can make a little difference in our world.

Optimism

Optimists achieve their goals much easier than pessimists. We are not destined to be optimistic or, on the contrary, to look at things from a pessimistic perspective. Moreover, optimism can be learned. How? Here are some steps:

- Learn from your mistakes
- Be aware of what has gone wrong and see how you will do things better next time
- Be able to see the positive aspects in all things
- It does not allow you to be negative
- When you have a negative thought, try to turn it into a positive one
- Think about everything you've done
- Do not consume energy with negative thoughts
- Think about how blessed you are

No matter how serious the circumstances are, there is something to be grateful for. There are always people in a worse situation than yours.

What is your answer to what life has to offer?

For most lawyers that feel as though they know everything, it is hard to accept that in certain situations, they might try to learn to face their own emotions and that they have to take the opportunity to follow a course to learn how to do that. What can you use a class for? It can give you the chance to find, in one place, as many tools as possible that can help you achieve something in life.

There will always be people who would prefer to spend money on holidays, valuables, or various forms of entertainment. However, a small group has discovered the reward of investing in their own development. We recommend that you take into consideration the possibility of participating in such development courses.

Although it seems very difficult to find a universally valid definition for happiness, we believe it is determined by the EC (Emotional Coefficient) and not by the CI (Intelligence Coefficient). All the courses we organized to support personal development are posted on the www.elawvation.com website.

You can sign up to receive our newsletter electronically.

We believe that our growth begins with the correct information and its application to everyday life.

Essential questions for a lawyer

Truth or justice?

It is said that the path of law is right, but is it also the road of the righteous? Although the truth is unique, we can all agree that, to a large extent, everyone has their righteousness. In any conflict, each person starts with the premise that he is right. The problem of winning remains, but this is another discussion, which would remove us from the intention of this book, which is to guide every lawyer to find his own truth in dialogue with his conscience, for this is the source from which to start in the fight for justice.

We are referring here to some sort of personal inner compass that checks the direction you are at a particular time. This is why we recommend that you establish, from time to time, a moment of grace in which you balance yourself and take an assessment so you can appreciate where you are at that moment.

Here we will guide you with a few landmarks to help you find your personal solution towards increasing your professional efficiency. It is not about making an extra effort. Please do not think you have to deal with an extra task other than what you already owe your clients. On the contrary, we are talking about personal gain in terms of time and energy. A gain that is quantified in self-care and which aims to increase your self-love.

Andreea: *was reading somewhere that when you love, it's like being in debt all the time. The more you love, the more your duty to love grows. But there is something to be added: when you introduce God into the equation, everything becomes easier. We are never alone. I don't know how faithful you are, but for me approaching God, or rather, reporting to God in the context of my problems, helped me. In fact, he was my helper, my salvation. Why do I say that? Because that is where the call came to my awakening from professional numbness. I became a pompous robot, sure of my own power, which erased God's.*

Although we come from a family where Christian education came first — our father is a priest — the profession of attorney has gained new value by cultivating a set of strong beliefs. We were talking earlier about the importance of the lawyer's role in society, but differently from how he is perceived today and the assumptions we make. I thought, at first, that we were in a position of power: we had all the rights. Then I understood that it was a professional flaw. No. Wrong! The lawyer is just a channel that must maintain high values and standards and keep his dignity so he can operate with righteousness.

Many lawyers misunderstand their role and are led by the opinions of their clients. It's a choice that makes you your own victim. It makes you come out defeated in the battle with your own ego. The one who loses will be your soul; a soul that has the right to peace, quiet, calm, freedom, divine joy, etc. Most of the time, the ego wins because it is aided by various resilient social beliefs and the perpetuation of a successful model in society that is based on strong competitive values.

Happy lawyers or productivity?

Is there any connection between happiness and productivity? We want to show lawyers at the beginning of their career, that there are tools that can be used to work, to be productive and, at the same time, to be happy. Most of the time, work and study are associated with the connotation of difficulty and sacrifice, but not with a sense of gratitude. But maybe by having a productive lifestyle, both personal and professional, gratitude should become a necessity.

We decided to help lawyers to be aware that maintaining a different lifestyle will help them to be more productive than they thought. We have collaborated with many lawyers and we can say that there are certain common problems.

How can you be more convincing, more credible but, at the same time, how will you manage to stay as professional as possible without invading the personal history of the client? How will you succeed or fight the mental stereotype of the interlocutor regarding your profession, the stereotype that is projected on you? First of all, you have to separate things. There is one thing you have to be aware of...the client's story is not your story.

His experience with other lawyers is just a part of his story. His misfortune up to that point must not affect you in any way. This requires your full attention, because the client will always tend to generalize, even if he doesn't realize he's doing it. Then how do you not interfere with his level of frustration? First of all, you have to clearly explain to the client that his past experience has nothing to do with the attorney's role itself; that the professional obligations are the same for any lawyer. Try to make him aware that, above all, the lawyer is a person like any other with education, characterizing his own consciousness. The moment you feel certain that you have clarified this aspect and that you are finally regarded as a Unique

Lawyer, you can move to the stage where you are gathering information to solve the client's problem.

Finally, we can conclude that every lawyer is responsible for his own well- being and how he manages the rapport with others. We want this book to bring something different in the context of this profession. We hope the lawyers who are at the beginning of the road, will find useful information here that will help improve and guide their entire career.

Focus on what you can do and stop thinking about what you're not ready to do. Every stage of a lawyer's career is different. Every situation and every client are different. You're dealing with a very diverse clientele, even if some matters are similar to others.

How to help your client?

Have you ever put yourself in the position of the man who sells a particular product? Most likely not. But lawyers, especially those specializing in business, trademark and similar domains, are selling services. As a lawyer, you do not sell products, but having the vision of a salesperson helps you to see things more easily from your client's perspective. Thinking differently means choosing a new perspective.

You have definitely met clients who say, "I'm not interested in explanations. I just want to solve the problem as soon as possible." Learn to reflect not only on the problem itself, but also on the affect that the problem has on the company's business in general. Such an approach allows you to ask key questions related to time, priorities, and resources, so that you can work more efficiently from the client's standpoint which is helpful to you.

It is known that there are several legal solutions in order to achieve various goals. The fact that you approach things from the perspective of your client will help you apply those solutions that suit him. When you are knowledgeable about your client and their business, you are not just in it for the exercise, it is an effective way of using a professional approach.

Usually, the lawyer tends to be limited by legal regulations, but a Unique Lawyer increases his coverage depending on the client's issue. When you take a holistic perspective on a case, you become a Unique Lawyer. You make the difference.

As doctors are required to treat each patient individually, lawyers must have a specific approach to each client. Every client is different.

Often, even lawyers with more practical experience use inflexible patterns while assessing and addressing situations. The personalized approach, tailored to the singular client, helps you find out what his resources are, including financials, in order to determine his costs and avoid that being the reason that his case is disrupted or blocked. You should also find out what the most upsetting issue is for your client, and what the consequences are if the matter is not resolved favorably or ends in an unexpected way. Use this information to establish priorities and objectives of the case with the client.

Once you have set your goals, you can gauge the resources you need such as the legislative basis, possibly the collaborators, the team, etc. The approach from the client's perspective makes a difference.

Very often, clients will not provide you with all the necessary information to solve a legal action and before you know it, you are in the middle of a case and you learn something new during a random discussion with your client. Having a clear strategy in mind and by clearly establishing what is most important to your client, you can guide the discussion to find the shortest and most effective way to solve the problem.

Put yourself in the client's place to be as close to their expectations as possible. Have you ever wondered what you are selling as a lawyer? The answer is safety; confidence that the client will get the best solution specific to his problem. But in order to do that, you have to identify his priorities. When your client is lost in detail, your role is to help him find the starting point in that case. Try to get your client to focus and build an effective communication relationship with you.

Of course, the lawyer is also required to be a good psychologist. This kind of skillset can help you provide quality professional services and give the client a high degree of satisfaction with the resolution of the case. Furthermore, a satisfied client will recommend you to others and your business will develop further.

Assume a silent commitment to your clients. It is your duty to create that energy field that attracts clientele. How do you do that? Maybe you've heard of the Law of Attraction. The more we are aware of your role, the more your responsibility will grow. People are not the same, and the tough ones need more understanding. But when you commit to providing a positive experience to each client, you will attract more business.

Besides the oath to obey the law, you also make a commitment to yourself (refer to previous chapter) of having a good practice by involving inner landmarks in harmony with your values, moral laws, and the ethical code of a professional attorney.

Competition or Contribution?

In the case of lawyers, some would say that, without a doubt, the competition is a part of their genetic code. But most of the time, the spirit of competition removes us from the joy that the fruit of our deeds gives us. We are aware that we are the ones who have the leading role in solving the legal problems of our clients.

Alone, this thought can lead to an over-inflated ego. But if we feel that this is nothing but a contribution to the good work of things, our ego kept in check. We can thus rejoice in a different way for what we are, and not for what we do. It is human nature to expect recognition when we succeed, but there are situations in which the lawyer works to their full potential and yet loses or cannot carry out a certain matter for reasons that are not his fault and thus does not receive the appreciation he deserves.

This is an example of a situation where you don't have to get knocked down by negative feelings or let the guilty feelings control you. In these instances, make sure that you have integrity, knowing that you did everything you could and then redirect your attention from the outside in. This way you can cope with the external pressure and you can maintain order in your inner universe.

It is like changing the direction of a river. If your intention is to give your best to help solve your client's problems, then you will be able to manage it with ease even when unsuccessful. The client will certainly perceive you differently than he was accustomed to or rethink the stereotypical image that he might have formed about the representatives of our profession. It's time to see things from another perspective. It is up to us to decide which direction we're heading towards that inner light. In my own experience, I have found that the line between a constructive and a destructive attitude is very subtle, no matter the subject.

The point is that you can perceive the same situation in many ways. The important thing is how and where you communicate it. When you get involved with all your heart, you will be able to communicate situations to your client that are not necessarily advantageous to them. The client must communicate from the outset what the legal possibilities are in relation to his situation, which will allow you to explain to him that there may be variables that can prevent him from getting the outcome he wants.

Many lawyers are wrong when they offer guarantees to their clients. This happens especially when they want to obtain a particular case at any cost. We have made that mistake. We were so sure of our strengths and on the certainty of the results that we did not calculate our risks very well and we did not analyze all the details at the beginning of the case.

Never offer free consultations! Communicate the situation as it is and try not to be disappointed when you do not obtain authorization from a client. There were situations where I invested time, and I even worked pro bono to get a case. In the end, something happened, and the collaboration was not completed through a warrant. Looking back, we realized it was better this way. It turns out that the client or that case was not exactly the best option to help build our reputation as lawyers. Even if certain situations seem different than you wished for, don't be disappointed and don't waste your energy on that case. Go ahead and turn your attention to situations that bring you actual benefits.

Alina: *During the coaching sessions we have offered, we have often found that bottlenecks are guided by our ego. This is the situation where the ego blinds you and you don't see another exit, another option, another potential client.*

Learn to give up something to make room for what is beneficial to the present moment of your career. Everyone has cases that are a good fit for their skills and passions, and they have to aim for them. You don't aim to get something that does not appeal to you. It may seem like an opportunity not to be missed, but it is good to grow progressively.

It doesn't seem motivational, but if you look at a different perspective, you will understand the exact meaning of this statement. Maybe you are made for much bigger things, for bigger challenges, for situations that few can solve. Why stay stuck in unproductive cases? Why interrupt the ascension of your career by wasting time and energy just for the sake of boosting your ego?

Andreea: *During school, we did not excel in the easy matters, it was the difficult subjects where we received higher grades. The difference was the motivation. The same goes for me in my professional career. Easy matters don't motivate me particularly, and that's not because of the money. I don't feel challenged. As long as I can remember, I've enjoyed strong confrontation, although I realize that before I was driven by ego most of the time. I let myself be carried so hard by the spirit of competition that I had moved away from myself. I heard them say: "That lawyer is hot, she's aggressive..." Later, when I realized the real meaning of those words, I woke up and I didn't recognize myself in those words.*

Eventually you will ask yourself, where the healthier place to find my motivation is? Simple…investigate yourself, and don't attach yourself to the disproportionate projection that your ego wants others to have about you. Be motivated by your human role in the profession you have chosen. Don't lose yourself on the altar of your career.

Benevolence — a term most often forgotten in the analysis of communication.

We have found in the most diverse situations that good will is a desire for well-being, and knowledge.

Sometimes, it may seem magical,

how someone seems to understand you perfectly even if you are speaking a different language. People still want to understand or be understood.

This desire to persuade can help others overcome obstacles.

Biased or impartial?

Even if it may seem like a truism, we think we need to express this clearly: a lawyer has to be impartial and must always have a neutral attitude towards the problem he needs to solve. It is true that the tendency of human nature is to judge, to seek justice and, in the case of our field, to follow a professional impulse that makes us get so involved that we become one with the case, and this leads to unwanted complications.

What would the lawyer-client relationship look like if the lawyer assumed an impartial role, and the client found his own solution? A Unique Lawyer clearly understands that his role is not to hand out justice, but to be a catalyst between the client and the law. In the "How to Help Your Client" section of this book, you can learn how to analyze a situation where the lawyer puts himself in the client's position to see what is expected of him. It's an exercise that allows you to see the case from a different perspective…that of the client.

The lawyer is meant to guide the client in accordance with the legal norms. The lawyer is the one who mediates a dispute, because those directly involved do not have the dynamism to overcome certain egos that can feed the conflict. In family matters, in business situations, in social matters, the Unique Lawyer is the one who tries to dispel the conflict.

Imagine what it would be like to use techniques in which, through precise questions, you have the ability to guide your client to find the solution themselves. We are not just referring to legal solutions and the way of law enforcement, but also to spiritual solutions, in a position to bring peace to the client.

What are the emotions that a client has that make him want to hire a lawyer? Can he solve his own conflict? Of course, we are referring to matters in which the human side could solve the problem. Here is a concrete example: We have a divorce case where both sides seem to be right. Each one appeals to a lawyer and waits for justice to be done. The human and professional role of the lawyer would be to help them solve the problem relationally without reaching the point of divorce. In this instance, the lawyer's valuable ability can intervene by being a good listener and a good counselor.

Fear of conflict or conscious management?

Conflict is part of our ego. It's hard to admit that, but you must. Follow your soul and listen to the rhythm of your heart.

Why do I say that? Because conflict imbalances us. Disagreement pushes us towards engaging an additional energy that we do not have, and this overload will show up in our health.

Andreea: *I knew how to fight to win. Most of the time, we are cowards because we are afraid to lose. When I was fighting, I only knew I had to prove I was good. I knew I would win. I was afraid of losing. I didn't know how to lose. But any loss is only part of your success.*

What I learned later helped me understand these things. I learned how to manage my own fears. Conflict is nothing more than a build-up of emotions, an unloaded energy. Like any energy, it can be used in a positive direction or in a negative direction. To diffuse the conflict, there are several techniques, either rational or emotional which, must often be combined.

There are situations in which conflict moves inside of us. The first step in managing any conflict, particularly an internal one, is awareness. Sometimes this is enough to make some of the discomfort instantly disappear. Think of it as emotions and different moods. They are part of you just as the other side is, because they are natural and deeply human. The way you manage them in the space you create for them is what makes the difference. At times like this, we offer you a few relaxation exercises (look for them in the last chapter of this book). From personal experience, we know that they are very effective in helping you change your mood.

Be a Unique Lawyer

Act differently to get different results

We need, we believe, to reposition the lawyer in relation to other factors involved in his professional practice. That is why we believe that the leadership role is best suited for a Unique Lawyer. The lawyer is a leader by definition. The profession we practice offers us a strategic position, forcing us to exercise this role.

Careful though! True leaders are those who know how to first lead themselves by managing their emotions and moods. Good lawyers see the human side and connect to the needs of others. To be a true leader, you first need to learn to observe the needs of those around you, especially your clients. That's the only way you can take responsibility for others. When you know you're responsible for others, you do your best to develop so you can cope with high demands.

There are classic examples of individuals that are responsible for the safety of others. When you are on a plane and you are traveling with a child, for instance, if an incident happens, you should first put the oxygen mask on yourself and then the child. The explanation is simple: if you lose consciousness, the child will not be able to put it on himself. Take care, therefore, of yourself, to be able to have others in your care.

Avoid blaming the environmental factors for what is happening to you.

Only we are responsible. We were taught to blame each other, to find excuses.

Andreea: *What I see often, especially in coaching sessions, is that lawyers expect to have different results without doing anything different. Here it is what I always say: Be responsible for the positive results (i.e. you deserve success), but also for the negative ones; they are just different ways of reaching success.*

Many times, I felt the business environment was like a jungle, in the context of the problems and conflicts I was exposed to when I represented the clients. But my tactics were to sneak in without leaving

traces in my soul. However, although I tried to erase them, their memory is there: it's like using an eraser; there's still a little trail.
At first, I was having a hard time communicating what other lawyers know, but when I was working towards an MBA, I heard about the concept of coaching and techniques that can help you achieve your goals. My objective was to communicate efficiently, so that my interns would be the best in professional terms and succeed in life, which happened. It is said that a true master is the one who is surpassed by his students. In our case, although the master can make a major contribution, the only person responsible for the success is the lawyer himself. He must be aware that his choices are affecting his professional and personal success. In our profession, the masters are important, but they represent only one resource. Take responsibility for your own success. So, if you think you need experience in a particular field, set your goal and act to reach it. Ask someone, document yourself, see who the best is in the field, dare to ask for help, do not wait for it to come to you. Do not expect anyone to notice that you lack an important skill, because at that time it is already too late.

Communicate the loss differently

There are several factors which can motivate a lawyer. The most important thing is the feeling of responsibility that they should have for their client and a respect for the law. The lawyer's mission is to protect his client, like a mother who defends her children. Think of your role as one that contributes to the good of others, but on the other hand, you can also be driven by the desire to demonstrate how good you are or how many good deeds you are doing. This is your ego, which has a role in motivating you to give your best.

When you are motivated by the ego, many lawyers tend to reveal the successes they have had in previous cases to their current clients. This strategy helps to establish credibility. A Unique Lawyer will also talk about different types of action, namely the contribution to various non-profit organizations, certain charities, etc., which moves the dialogue to a different level of communication that touches that part of the clients' soul that resonates with these aspects. Why not consolidate credibility in this way? Our inner profile and our public image are built on the foundation of our good deeds, whether they are stimulated by genuine care or the need for significance.

The test with our inner witnesses

Think of yourself as a witness. Be honest with yourself and evaluate your- self. Notice if you're satisfied with yourself. Surely, we all want to be successful, but few are ready to act in this direction, to enter this dance. And in law, like in any other field, when you want more you have to give more. The important thing is not what you do, but how you do it.

Alina: *Often we are tempted to reach extremes. I remember in college; I was studying before the session and getting exhausted on the last hundred meters. I could not do this throughout my career and not only because I would no longer have my youth and the necessary energy, but I knew I was responsible for others, not just for me.*

When you feel responsible for others, this changes the rules of the game. You can't afford to play with other people's lives. There's a dialogue with yourself. The sense of responsibility makes us more attentive to ourselves, spurs us to self-analysis, and urges us to act in the most appropriate direction, both for ourselves and for others.

A man who feels responsible not only for himself, but also for the fate of others, cannot be an impulsive individual. On the contrary, it takes introspection, rationality, and a continuous effort of self-knowledge. Don't hide from yourself. Be unique and authentic. Be yourself. You can fool someone, you can fool everyone for a while, but you can't fool everyone all the time. The same happens when you display a personal image that is incongruent with your own self. In the end, you can't fool anyone by mimicking what you are not.

Once you enter the community of lawyers, you will quickly notice that, for many of your peers, appearances matter. The image and the way you are presented comes at a great price and it is vital to know how to sell yourself well in a competitive society. In the long run, you will need to know how to win, as there are those professionals who know how to present something as more than a form without merit. Those who support their image with real skills and abilities, duplicated by professional and human consciousness at the same time.

Take that witness of your own consciousness and act responsibly. Before you make a confession about yourself, I would advise you to have a talk with your "witnesses" inside. Make sure you have all the evidence to prove what you're proposing. If you've entered the dance, then dance. You cannot have all the evidence from the beginning – that is, resources, knowledge, and experience. Gather them, study, ask your colleagues for help, communicate what you need and then act. Plead your case and win!

Adopt a winning mentality

The most widespread idea is that a good lawyer is also a good actor. In truth, there is a need for such a talent in order to be successful in this profession. But the quasi-unanimous perception refers to the ability of the lawyer to uphold things he knows are not true. And even if it is true that life can be considered a scene, it is good to acknowledge the role you play in your own conscience arena. Not everything is measured by the amount of an invoice. Sometimes things are measured through inner peace in relation to the effort made.

In our profession it is hard to keep yourself centered on your values when you enter into relationships with different people who do not have the same values as yours. Set your standard and performance level and act smart. Don't give up. Remember what Aristotle said: "The winners do not give up, and those who give up do not become winners."

Don't assign yourself the failures

A common mistake is to feel guilty about lost lawsuits, even though you know you've done all you could. When you know you have done everything possible, but for various reasons you haven't won, try to evaluate yourself honestly and observe yourself without a sense of guilt. The one who cannot bear to lose has an ego problem, manifested by a state of anxiety. In fact, no one has ever succeeded without having lost.

Evaluate yourself and observe your weaknesses. You must weigh every weakness and learn from the mistakes made. Do not succumb to the tendency to blame those around you, especially when you have to justify failure in front of the client. The important thing for your conscience is to be honest with others, to find the right way to communicate negative results. If you think you do not have the most effective tools in this regard or do not consider that there is room for improvement in your strategies of interconnection with clients, we suggest that you carefully go through the next chapter, dedicated to the problems of communication.

Relationship Master- Lawyer Trainee

For us, one of the most difficult parts of our professional activity was related to the management of the relationship with the intern lawyers. Communicating with them seemed impossible. We had great expectations of them, but not the patience to explain those expectations to ensure their understanding.

The truth is that the emotional factor is very important when relating with a person who has less experience than you. I have to confess that at first, we did not have the ability to effectively manage the relationship with interns, although we tried. Eventually, we managed to convey the information to the best of our ability, but with too much effort, with too much energy consumed.

There are also renowned lawyers who have the patience to relate to their interns. Perhaps they can be considered lawyers of another era. The lawyers today have more work and less time to devote themselves to trainees. This is probably because today's pace is different, and the expectations are higher. It is imperative that we do all we can to help the development of professional and personal counsel of young lawyers.

We had a very difficult time in this because we had not been trained in this area, nor did we have the chance to read a book like the one you are now reading that is dedicated to the personal development of lawyers.

From our research before writing this book, we discovered that this is the first personal development book especially designed for lawyers.

The need to personally develop the team

Many informed employers understand the necessity of developing a team and know that work and home are linked. For example, they send their employees to workshops, team-building exercises, and other types of trainings that will help improve professional success and also the quality of personal life. However, most employers do not realize how important this link is and, consequently, employees are left to figure out how to maintain the balance between their private life and professional life and how to take responsibility to develop and maintain enthusiasm. Advocates should be happy when other lawyers invest in personal training, because happy and dynamic people are much more productive.

Inspire by Personal Example

The basis of any suffering is a positive lesson. I worked, at one point, with a person obsessed with the fact that she felt helpless and alone in everything she did. It was her inner child, used to loneliness and feeling like a victim. Growing up without her parents caused her to form comfortable behavioral patterns. Thus, she endeavored to attract attention to herself.

As I have said in previous chapters, we believe that modesty is an essential quality. But it is no less true that people dedicate themselves to good deeds and great causes by often following the example of others. Inspire others by your example. Be a different kind of mentor; one who transfers something from himself to another person. Something about your soul and your mind should pour into someone else's life and, in the end, our world.

We were told that we are not teachers and that we must instead learn from others. We were accustomed to being restrained, to not being able to express our- selves. In a word, there was a block from the divine source that springs from every human being. Permission to let the divine spark and go free means open- ness and trust. If our intention is to shape a different world in which each of us has a unique contribution, then we will become aware of the responsibility of making it possible for this openness to lead to a better world for all of us.

It is not that simple. Fears and limitations in this context are incredible. It is like trying to change the course of a river. This is what happens to an idea that you have, with an action that springs from your soul that remains hidden because of fear. Let it spring forth. They say we must begin, and God will continue. The important thing is to listen to your inner being, to act in accordance with yourself. In this way, you are staying connected with yourself and you will be different.

We would like to emphasize here that the divine part of each of us has been placed there, either for ourselves or for another person. You will become aware of how important you are, as a human being, when you realize that you are part of something greater than yourself and that you have a meaningful contribution to the common good. But don't wait for immediate gratitude. You don't need anyone's validation to be yourself.

Everything flows, says the aphorism attributed to Heraclitus. Everything flows naturally, aligns naturally. From nature, we learn how to behave, how to embrace the thought of being authentic. Although it seems very easy, being natural is rather a forgotten ability in today's society. In essence, people are different. Modern society has leveled them and created well-aligned robots who are doing their job efficiently.

Through this book, we would like to show you the possibility of existence after another paradigm, of "being different". In this way, we want to approach the authentic nature of your soul. We believe that this paradigm will help you go beyond appearances, to return to yourself, to connect with yourself and to discover the truth that resides in your being, as the happy Augustine said.

Push aside the labels you have attached in different contexts (family, friends, and society). You do not aim to be different from your own self. You do not want to be different from your uniqueness, your singular truth. It is easy. When you get to be connected with yourself, with your truth, you see everything in a new light. You feel how suddenly a dark curtain has been removed from your eyes. You can see how a different world, a new horizon opens to you and it is like you have wings and can explore many things, places, beautiful forests, flowers, shapes, and colors. You feel as if you would like to instantly explore the entire universe. But your inner universe is left undone, unexplored, untouched. Perhaps the time has come for you to give it life, to touch it as you would if you had a magic wand.

Give life to your inner resources and admit it if you still feel that terrible need to be recognized, to be important. Only then can you understand that you are, in fact, important to your authentic self. Not as you present yourself to others, wrapped in a beautiful wrapper, betting on the fascination of the advertising message that promotes you.

The world we live in is troubling us with all sorts of meanings, of misunderstandings, in fact, of confusion. Slaves to the labels, stereotypes, we all find ourselves in the same context that we want to escape as soon as possible. Rightly we want to get away, but maybe we needed to get to this stage in order to realize that this is not us. That this artificial landscape is not where we should abide.

To understand how easily you gave up what was given to you, stop for a moment and make a list of things you have given up, although you did not want to. Make another list of things you want to give up and you think you cannot.

Write the two lists below:

....	....
....	....
....	....
....	....

Now you start to tidy up and follow the proper directions in your life. It is as if the sun came out and it starts shining on new portions of your world. It is a different approach, which will give you more and more meaning in your personal life.

The Core of a Unique Lawyer: The confidence he inspires in others

Throughout our career, we have always bet on a path whose importance in the economy of success we rediscover every day, with each new case, with each challenge at hand. This is about the personal capital of credibility that our name (our brand, in fact) generates in the market of those who practice law. I understand, as the years have passed, that success in this profession is not measured only in the number of cases won in court or at the negotiating table. That the career of a successful lawyer is the sum of all the achievements and lessons that he learned from defeats. That, beyond the inherent ups and downs remains the constant of a prestigious name, gained with great toil and maintained with even greater efforts. We believe that a prerequisite condition of this prestige represents the credibility of our name.

How do we build the personal capital of credibility in this vocation that we have chosen? We will tell you that from the beginning that it was not a leap, but a process. We are not talking about a fight won, but a string of wars that we all face. It is the task for everyone to establish their own way forward.

Our purpose is to present a few lines; some principles that have guided us and which have quickly shown their importance. What is your role? How can you begin to act, specifically, to build this asset of a prestigious name, a credible brand? We suggest, in the following lines, a few steps that we firmly believe can help you in this direction.

- **Determine who you want to be, how you want to be treated and what kind of clients you want to have. Do not accept anything else. Give up a little to win more. Stay on that line you are positioning and investing in yourself one hundred percent.**
- **Dare to be more than a lawyer; be a different kind of lawyer! Activate a different mindset: think like a businessman! Invest in your business to make it profitable. Want to position yourself in the top? Give up habits and convictions that do not align with your position.**
- **Create a valuable portfolio, work with people who can talk well about you, about your professional skills and about your human value. Speak to your clients about the successes you have had, let go of false modesty and display your merits.**

Andreea: *I know lawyers who lose valuable clients because they do not assume a position corresponding to their level of competence. A Unique Lawyer knows how to position himself where he belongs and does it gracefully, without disturbing or emitting any trace of arrogance. Honesty about ourselves puts the cornerstone in the building of a relationship between us and our clients based on trust and mutual respect.*

- **Do not burn bridges or position yourself at a level you have not yet reached. You could impress people for a moment, but in the long run, you could experience suffering at a level of the subconscious which does not belong to you. In addition, there will always be a boomerang effect. I have heard many client complaints about the hypocritical attitude of the lawyers with whom they had collaborated. That is why we consider such a self-correct valuation, emanating from a good self-knowledge.**
- **Do not evaluate yourself solely on the basis of your achievements or successes. You may gain outstanding performance on a professional level and yet you will not get the sympathy of your clients. It will be harder, therefore, to create a genuine connection with your clients or potential clients. Something extra is needed; personal charisma. Our rational side can guarantee decency and effective communication, but a harmonious inter-human relationship is established both at the conscious level and in planes of the subconscious.**
- **Enable your "indoor radar" to bring harmony to your clients. You will meet different client typologies in your career. A Unique Lawyer will know how to accurately appreciate what kind of personality traits are needed at one moment or another. He will gracefully and delicately enter his client's world and invite him into his own.**

Since ancient times, four typologies of personality have been established: sanguine, phlegmatic, choleric, and melancholic. These types of personalities are, to a lesser or greater extent, present in each of us and define the way we think, feel, and address reality. The characteristics of the four typologies are well known. However, we found it useful to have a brief review of them, as a useful tool that you can have at your fingertips when preparing a first meeting with a potential client.

Sanguine

The sanguine personality is characterized by spontaneity, optimism, enthusiasm, energy at maximum rates, flexibility in the way of thinking, impulsiveness, and curiosity. All these traits are associated with certain genes influenced by the dopamine levels present in our system. Individuals predominantly sanguine usually have expressive faces. Their favorite words are "adventure", "energy", "new", "fun", "action", and "journey".

Phlegmatic

The personalities of the phlegmatic type are mainly defined by their social skills, by the ability to express their feelings and to *read* other people by the expression on their face and their body language. The phlegmatic is great at linking different facts and have the ability to see the overall picture of a problem or situation. They have a great capacity for empathy. They know how to nurse others and are agreeable and emotionally expressive. Some of these personality traits are related to estrogen, which is present in both women and men. Physically, the phlegmatic has smooth skin, full lips, round faces, and small noses. Their favorite words are "passion", "passionate", "tenderness", and "sweet".

Choleric

The choleric type (hot-tempered) is associated with the level of testosterone in the body, which is also present in both men and women. Choleric people are direct and focused on the task that they have to accomplish. They are tough, analytical, and logical and they have a great capacity to develop strategies. They are very brave and they like competition. Physically, they often have square jaws, big cheekbones, and wide foreheads. They often use words like *intelligence, ambition, and challenge.*

Melancholic

Those belonging to the melancholic type tend to be calm, loyal, and orderly. Melancholic people are cautious and always behave according to the conventional rules of society. This type of personality is linked to our serotonin level. The favorite words of melancholic people are *family, loyal, respect, care, values, and morale.*

Knowing the overall characteristic of each typology, you can easily sketch a portrait of your speaker, drawn in the dominant characteristics of one type or another. Observe the predominant traits of your client and adapt your type of approach so that you can create a harmonious working relationship.

Communication Typologies in NLP

From a modern perspective, in the context of the science of human behavior, Neurolinguistic Programming (NLP), states that there are certain types of communication and certain human typologies: visual, auditory, kinesthetic, and olfactory and taste. In negotiations, "VAK Technique" (visual, auditory, kinesthetic) is very often used. That is why it is important to familiarize ourselves with these typologies; to achieve our objectives more easily.

Each of these presets may be found in different doses, and all these typologies might be observed in some individuals, but only one will prevail. Studies on this subject have shown that the predominant type is the visual one.

- A *visual* client will respond to you when you speak to them in descriptive images, using expressions like: "Can you imagine what this situation will look like?"
- The *auditory* client responds when you formulate the same question differently: for example, "How does this proposal sound?".

- With the *kinesthetic* client, you should address him with a delicate touch or acknowledge them by a delicate movement of your body.

Don't forget that in all these exercises, optimizing the communication relationship with your clients, it is fundamental to bring, beyond the information presented here, your personal energy. In fact, the same scheme of human typologies in NLP can also apply to you. Therefore, the premise of establishing an effective communication relationship lies first in good observation and self-knowledge.

Don't forget that we are all unique and different.

Between Victory and Fee: The art of becoming and remaining a successful lawyer

We are all motivated, in this profession, by two fundamental things. Even if the attraction force of these two poles varies from man to man and even on a case-by-case basis. It is, on the one hand, about the idea of victory and, on the other, the prospect of a satisfactory fee.

After a few years of accumulated experience, we have wondered, as you probably do, what remains ultimately. Is it following many solved cases or a smaller or larger case of victories or is it collecting substantial funds? What is the continuous and constant source of professional satisfaction for a lawyer; or for a human for that matter?

We believe that, beyond the check of the causes gained and the checks received, the consciousness of professional success is found. Know that you are a successful lawyer and that it stands in your power to maintain this status. Let us return, however, to the first sources of satisfaction that any lawyer at the beginning of his career will experience. Victory vs. fee, both together. These two targets are as real as possible in the mind-set of lawyers.

Why Victory First of All?

The very purpose of the lawyer is described as being in the service of his client, acting, of course, within the limits of the law. On the other hand, it would be unrealistic to ask a lawyer to feed his enthusiasm and energy exclusively with the victor's laurels. Significant is the fact that the ancient Greeks, for example, share sporting events in two categories: those considered sacred, where the trophy consisted exclusively of a wreath of laurel or olive and thematic branches, and on the other hand the winners were rewarded with material possessions.

Unfortunately, most lawyers are not familiar with the science of marketing and sales. They do not know how to value their work, how to really convey the work and effort it takes to solve a matter.

Andreea: I remember this scenario at a time in my career when the most important thing seemed to be the result. I was fascinated with a case and put a bet first with myself that I would emerge victorious. Eventually, I woke up like, bridge already crossed, my client would relax when the time of the fee was to be paid off. The negotiations would start, even though it could not have been something like that at the time. The satisfaction of victory turns, then, in pure frustration.

Why the fee first of all?

Because we simply do not live in a world of embodied ideals in our daily reality! The work of the lawyer assumes a considerable responsibility, and his revenues are, anywhere in the world, above average.

Unfortunately, today there are many lawyers who consider the goal of victory as secondary or even consider winning the cause of the amount of the fee charged. From here, inevitably, tensions occur between him and the client. The latter feels at a subtle level a hidden agenda, develops distrust in his lawyer, and may tend to create bottlenecks in paying the fee. Because the situations of this kind are not exceptions to the rule, our society has developed various stereotypes about this profession and preconceived ideas only to shadow the merits of many lawyers who dedicate themselves to their work in a real way.

Unique Lawyers - Beyond the victory at all costs, beyond the primacy of the massive fee

We believe that the Unique Lawyer model we propose will no longer develop such false dilemmas, because he assumes a different way of action. A Unique Lawyer shares something in common with all successful businessmen, he has a clear goal, in our case, solving the client's problem.

When you set a goal, you can count on the fact that generally the result is measurable. In our case, having to deal with a diligent profession, measuring the results consists of all the actions to be undertaken in solving the case, knowing that it is very important to communicate them, because the lawyer-client relationship can fall apart, just like any relationship, due to lack of communication. As a strategy to remember, we suggest that when you set a goal, set it clearly together with the path of obtaining results, as well as the methodology of measuring them.

Purpose

As we continue on the topic of goal setting, it is preferable to formulate the objectives that you propose to be articulated in order to achieve a purpose in a more general sense or, rather, generously. Often, the goal is empowered by a powerful motivational source, depending on the psyche of each individual involved.

It is not, however, as you would expect of setting a deeply personal, individual purpose in the last instance. In our case, the purpose of a Unique Lawyer is rather the result of the client's purpose.

If the one who crosses your office threshold is interested exclusively in gaining victory, your goal will follow, and you will collect a fair fee.

We know that it is a sensitive theme for many colleagues, but the truth is that we can no longer live with the mask of hypocrisy, as long as we are talking about a right earned through honest effort. Spiritually, this way of thinking only opens your heart more and urges you to work with dedication in the spirit of truth, of law. So, we invite you to be honest with yourself, to communicate your own truth and to ask for a fair fee for the work rendered on behalf of your client, and you will notice that no more blockages will appear in your report.

This last aspect is not neglected at all. Of course, in general, any professional deserves to be compensated depending on the effort made and the value of his work. Beyond that, a Unique Lawyer will know how to evaluate in measurable terms what you might call a rating or market. Because he has worked diligently to build a prestigious name in this business, he will not hesitate to properly value himself to all parties involved.

More than a winning case or a cash fee, it's about the strength of your own reputation that tells about your own brand, built with so much effort.

But whatever your short-term purpose is, we strongly recommend that you always try to put quality into your actions. The value of your personal brand is weighed both in relation to your client, as well as in the quality of your services in your degree of involvement. You will find, after years of sustained efforts, that reaching the top is not the same as knowing how to keep yourself there. After all, the most spectacular falls are those from the top of the pyramid, not the ones at the base. Therefore, we believe that the most valuable experience is not so much gained from the top position, but how many jumps you made to get there.

To achieve your goal of maintaining the prestigious level you have attained, we recommend that you check in with yourself to determine your degree of involvement that you are willing to prove. You will remain at the top if you understand that involvement does not mean personal sacrifice and that the purpose of keeping your inner balance and your health is the first priority.

Andreea: *I remember myself, back when I was getting involved in pretty complicated files, which involved displacements, drafting, studying, besides other pressing tasks that I didn't know how to prioritize*

and manage at that time (I was not a Unique Lawyer). Eventually, the immediate result translates into various physical ailments.
The case was totally ripping me off, making me come out of it, and the worst part was I wasn't even aware of it. In fact, I could not see the truth, I did not have that dialogue with myself, which would have brought clarity and, certainly, milder solutions for my soul. My ego couldn't afford to let me fail; I was only relying on myself. I was not aware that, I had a precious purpose: my own health.

How can you counteract, you may ask, this risk of burn-out, so endemic in our field? We offer you another ingredient in this respect:

Your action plans

A Unique Lawyer knows exactly what he is after because he has a clearly formulated purpose, and from here he can establish a plan of action to follow step by step. In this phase, your potential for focusing is very important. Stay focused on the lens, but don't do it rigidly! Flexibility gives you the freedom to be open to alternative or helpful solutions and enable you to cope with unforeseen situations that can occur anytime along the way. Here, as a suggestion, are a few steps to go through:

Formulate clear questions and try to provide answers

- What do I have to do?
- What is the top priority?
- Do I have the necessary resources (knowledge, expertise, etc.) to personally handle or collaborate on this dossier?
- Is it possible to achieve the objective of the case legally? Be honest with yourself and your client.
- Do I have the time it will require to take over and carry out this case? Consider your schedule, and the other files you are in charge of. See, in this respect, the chapter on time management.
- Does my action plan depend, somehow, on third parties or institutions? Consider these issues before you retrieve a file.

Consider the aspects of the relationship you can build with your client.

- Establish the professional rapport that you consider to be the best one to develop with one client or another (see chapter on communication). Beyond the professional relationship, there is always a human relationship, on a personal level.
- In this context, you know whom you are dealing with, which client is in front of you, what energy it requires, what communication possibilities exist. Broadly, it is good to consider the kind of person you are going to work with. All these aspects will allow you to easily manage the future lawyer-client relationship so you can talk about a harmonious collaboration.

Don't hesitate to put technology to work to your advantage.

- Make a list in your calendar. We use, for example, Google forms and Google Docs, which helps us a lot to plan our actions effectively. Attention! Don't forget an essential factor for the success of your actions: yourself!
- Your personal program to maintain a satisfactory physical and mental state, your energy balance must be at the top of your list of priorities. That's the only way to get the maximum yield. You can include, in your To Do List, a section reserved for personal actions (see chapter on health).

The status of our profession: Between a simple lawyer and a businessperson

Times change and the attorney profession can only keep up with this change. We hear business mentioned more often when speaking about the guild of Lawyers. Do we have to worry about this, to take it as a sign of decency in another area that, once, enjoyed prestige and high attire? Not at all, we think. On the contrary, in these new times – there are also new people! And, we also say, new vision, new methods of action and involvement in our professional life and in the life of the community. The lawyer's profession, with its prestigious history, could not make a discordant note.

Law practice: a business?

Of course, why should we be intimidated by this title? On the one hand, avoiding the term can find its roots in the years of communism, loaded with preconceived ideas and ideological propaganda. Our society has surpassed, however, that era, so no one believes today that doing business in law, after investing effort and years of studying to perfection, can be an immoral thing. It would be naive to believe that the only concern and all the energy of a lawyer is focused exclusively on the defense of their clients, without paying any attention to the financial gain. Everything is that the latter does not receive such a measure as to interfere with the code of ethics of our guild.

On the other hand, many people exercise their profession under the threat of a veritable sword of Damocles represented by the perspective of financial failure. We know many lawyers who have a hard time thinking about this financial issue and therefore tend to neglect it. They seem to have forgotten that one of the principles that governs our profession is that of freedom. Yes, our profession is liberal, and independent; which is why we should take the helm to ensure the success of our profession and also look into the financial aspects of our business.

In order to practice, lawyers need an office, they need employees, collaborators who have to pay and make monthly expenses for fulfilling their obligations. So, as you can easily observe, there is an input (fees) but also an output (expenses). The tendency now is to allow lawyers to do some sort of promotion which involves other investments.

Alina: *I remember that, at the beginning of my career, I was reinvesting part of the income in business trips, conferences, and participation in different networking sites to find new clients. All these expenses hang in the balance and there's no way to admit that, from this point of view, you own a business. That's why I think it's very good if early on, you start to consider yourself a businessman or a businesswoman!*

But what does it entail to have your own business?

- Get involved, instruct, and investigate this financial reality! Even if you're not a lawyer specializing in finance or taxes, it's good to have the minimum of information to keep your business afloat. Also, if you want your business to grow, this dimension is fundamental. Make a list of monthly expenses and establish an investment budget to generate new clients. Notice how much you invest and how much you earn. We know many colleagues who complain that they have no new clients but do nothing about it. They are not accustomed to investing in promoting their own activity because they do not see it as a business.
- The more you know about the world of finance, the freer you will be, and you will not have to depend on others. Of course, it involves an extra effort, an investment of time and energy in yourself. We assure you that, in the medium and long term, all this toil will show its fruit and the investment in your business will promptly bring you profit – both financially and prestigiously.

On the other hand, we believe that an honest and persevering professional, as is the Unique Lawyer, has no reason to avoid the idea of prosperity. Prosperity is naturally part of our life when we know how to make room for it and when we act on it. It is a reward for our competences and effort, and not about a usurped right.

Furthermore, we learned, after years of experience and after a careful examination of ourselves, that prosperity is not just about money. That it can also be a state in which we are, or are not at some point, and to activate this condition in our lives, we do not have to move mountains. All we have to do is follow, with determination, a string of small actions.

Andreea: *For me, living prosperously means having my gym where I do my daily exercises, and having time for massages and spa treatments. Still in my idea of prosperity enter, however, and the gesture of offering help whenever I am in the least. My heart also rejoices if I succeed in having moments where I can smile for no particular reason, if I can find the respite of practicing daily meditation and living mindfully. To read when I want to, know what I don't like and what I like, what I can accept and what I cannot. I love the presence of flowers in my home and an atmosphere of harmony around me, I love to travel...*

Openness to prosperity can be described, from another perspective, as a certain type of personal vibration. When we create this vibration in our lives, we attract another similar vibration, which can be translated, in our case, by attracting numerous clients, through more professional experiences to provide us with satisfaction, as well as through a financial abundance. Remember, however, in all these endeavors, the laws of the universe that say that you cannot receive if you do not give, respect the flow and be generous. Give up some to gain more.

For example, within the *Unique Be Different* foundation, we propose to encourage lawyers to contribute to humanitarian projects, thus enabling them to participate in generous actions. I found, in this sense, inspiration in a TV show that I watched many years ago. Some lawyers from the UK volunteered to build a village of homes for the elderly. This gesture impressed us very much and made us reflect. Such disinterested actions have the gift to make us rediscover the human side of us. We believe that lawyers need to participate in these gestures to revise their stereotyped image in our society, which considers them exclusively interested in the financial aspect of their profession.

I said before that prosperity translates into the luxury of allowing us, at least for certain periods of time, to do what we like, to devote ourselves to things that we enjoy and are passionate about. But that goes for our career as well. Take a few moments of leisure and meditate on this issue: is what you like or think about, first of all, the financial gain?

I have met many colleagues who complain they have no clients; that they want more and that they are not happy with their lives. I wasted so much time thinking intensely about this, without realizing that it enhances this state of fact even only through the energy of their thoughts. They do not realize that it stands in their power to change this ratio of strengths. And that the first step would be to try to start thinking differently, asking questions and looking for new solutions from a new perspective, ascending into a new paradigm, developing a new mindset:

- Do I like what I do?
- How do I wish to live?
- What kind of clients do I want?
- What cases do I want to work on?
- How can I organize myself better?
- How can I ask for help to get what I want?

We believe that these are just a few questions that can redirect you towards your goals and help you get out of the state of tension in which daily challenges throw you at some point. I understand, in our career, that stress cancelling leaves room for the possibility to perform in full freedom, in harmony with what distinguishes each and every one of us and makes us unique.

We have found, over the years of professional experience, that large goals can be achieved through sustained effort, starting with small steps and going to breathtaking distances. Try to dedicate yourself to act this way and notice what changes in your life!

Invest to win! As in any business, there are, and in our case, three important variables to consider:

- Liquidity
- Profitability
- Risk

Take the three points and evaluate your present financial situation before you act to achieve your long-term financial goals. We understand that it may seem difficult, but we know that you can be helped in this matter. In the *Unique Lawyer System*, you will receive more tools and learn more concrete steps to- wards success, well studied and applied in practice.

No one is born with the gene of success. Acceptance and competence for success is learned. Here is an extremely important lesson in the learning of this art. There are so called factors of success that can prove fundamental in your decisions.

Therefore, remember:

- When you want more, you need to invest more. This is a key principle in the business world. Because we are convinced of the necessity of affirming an innovative law practice model, which we have called the *Unique Lawyer System*, we remind you that, within this investment, you enter and invest in yourself.
- Remember that you cannot have different results if you do not act differently! Before deciding, consider the above recommendations, concentrated in the OSA principle: *Objective* (What do I Want?), *Purpose* (What do I want this for?), *Action* (What should I do to get this?). This scheme will help you orient more efficiently and will free you from your concerns aimed at distracting you from your objective.
- Include, within your business plan, a ritual of gratitude for what you want to create. A thank you to the universe for what we are about to achieve. It is important that you have faith in what you plan to achieve and trust that you will succeed.

Andreea: I*n my coaching sessions to which a variety of people participated in the business environment, there were repeatedly suppositions initially that there were financial bottlenecks, although the undertaken actions seemed to be correct. It was missing, however, an important element. In his subconscious, my client had a program that was not in harmony with his objective. Moreover, he was convinced* *that he was not worthy of success. To be successful was, for him, a foreign and cold term: it didn't belong to him and he didn't accept it. I worked for a peri- od of time on this particular issue and things changed a lot, for the better.*

- The discipline factor is able to bring us back to ourselves when the daily grind pulls us off our own path to success. Discipline, as we like to assert, is the mother of self-esteem. The more disciplined you are, the faster you will fulfill your goals and your path to success will be smoother and everything will flow into harmony.

To conclude, we will return to the initial question: Advocate for the *Unique Lawyer System* – A simple lawyer or a businessman? Of course, everything depends essentially on what everyone wants and their own options. But we are convinced that in our world so changing and challenging, lawyers are among the most entitled to act in the business environment.

We've often been asked how we manage to do so many things. We believe, now, by looking back, that if we did not respect, from the outset, some essential principles and if we did not plant the seeds in the garden of our own success, we would not have come to know the beauty of success.

CHAPTER 3

DIALOGUE

People talk a lot about communication, but they communicate a lot less.

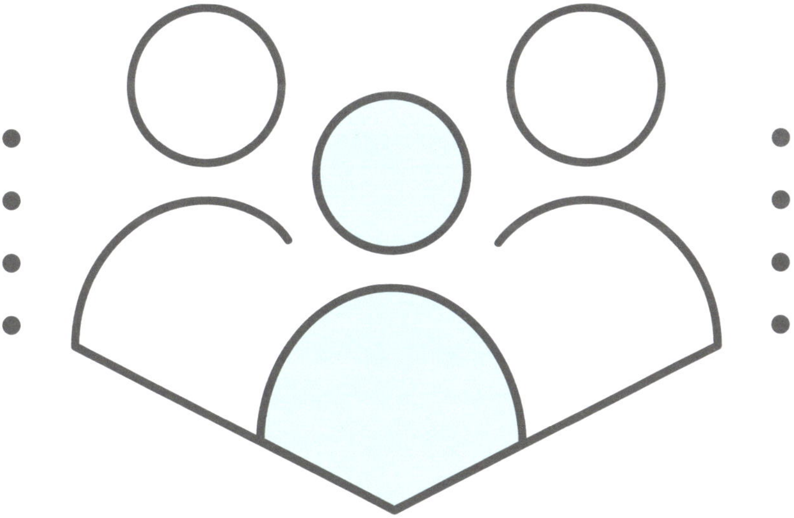

I CAN

To communicate is to get the truth out **to the light...**

Chapter 3
Communication

What is communication?

Communication is a concept theorized in the same way that covers our interaction with others, which includes ordinary conversation, persuasion, training, and negotiation. Communication is actually a cycle or a loop, involving at least two people. When communicating with another person, you receive their message and react with your own thoughts and feelings.

But communication is not just words. You communicate through words by tone of voice and nonverbally through postures, gestures, and expressions. Communication is a permanent flow. A message is transmitted even when you say nothing and stay still. So, communication involves a message that goes from one person to another.

How do you know if the message you want to transmit coincides with the received message? You have probably had a situation in which you happened to make a neutral remark to someone, and then discover with amazement that the converser interpreted your words differently. How can you be sure that the other person understands exactly what you intended to tell him?

We believe that the answer to many problems or communication jams that you have encountered, both in your personal life and in your professional activity, is in your eagerness to inform yourself, to study, to know more.

On the one hand, this thirst for knowledge must be quenched externally: read, search, study, instruction. On the other hand, the theory itself is not enough. It is desirable to show availability for change, to search for those solutions designed to make us communicate more efficiently and more deeply with other people. And then it takes an exploration of our personal knowledge. How do you communicate with others? What does it mean for you to communicate? What prevents you, in certain situations, from communicating efficiently? How can you improve your communication skills? How can this help you in your professional activity but also in your personal life?

Here are a number of questions that a good professional, a Unique Lawyer in our case, should try to provide satisfactory answers for so that his life can change for the better.

Types of communication

1 Verbal language

Life in a community involves communicating with others and language helps us achieve this. Language and the excellent design of the human being makes our inner world become visible, sound-perceivable, tangible to others. It allows us to share experiences of the most diverse and to communicate abstract ideas, to understand and to be understood.

Language gives us an amazing freedom within certain boundaries. We do not necessarily restrict our thoughts but limit their expression to others and this can lead to misunderstandings in both directions. First, the words we use may be inappropriate to describe our thoughts and, second, the others may not confer the same significance that we give to certain words, because each has their own vision of life and, it can therefore assign different meanings to some verbal expressions. Language is shared by everyone, but the significance is created individually, and it may not appear the same to everyone. Through language we communicate events and experiences with the help of instruments that derive from the structure and the way to build their own language, rather than from the experience that generates communication through language.

Language is more than a means of transmitting information. It is also a special way that individuals express themselves (verbal conduct) involving various activities such as speech, obedience, exchange of ideas, retention of sound messages, reproduction or translation. Language is a tool we use in creating our reality. It helps us to make a faithful assessment of how we see a specific situation.

2 Congruence in communication

Congruent means aligning beliefs, values, skills and actions, so that words become facts. Congruent also means being in relation to yourself. More specifically, it refers to the ability of the individual to be himself, whatever the feelings they have at some point towards his interlocutor.

In our case, for instance, if as a lawyer you act *as if* you respect your client, *as if* you care about him, *as if* you are judging him, *as if* you accept him as he is, you'll notice how your client will perceive the difference between expressing imitation or artificiality of communication.

The advantages of a congruent communication:

The more congruent a person can prove to be, the more it is possible that his or her messages are lacking in obscure and ambiguous significance, to be better understood by the other. The clearer your communication is, the more likely the other speaker will respond with clarity to you. Even if our client does not have everything congruent in his experience with the topic at hand, his answer will be much clearer than if he had received ambiguous messages from you. The more congruent you are the better, you will express yourself in a more authentic manner that you think about the subject in question, and the more you will be willing to listen to your client.

Therefore, you will come across less defensively, the more you will be able to listen in a more appropriate manner to what your conversation partner tells you.

For the client, the fact of feeling understood means that the lawyer has a positive consideration towards him, to be authentic, congruent and empathetic. Successful people know that all elements of communication must be in harmony and not cancel each other out. It means doing what you say and saying what you are doing. In this way, you're convincing or congruent. To speak in a fast pace and, at the same time, gesture slowly is an example of a loss of harmony in communication. Another example is to talk about a nice or pleasant thing and have a facial expression of discontent. This phenomenon is called incongruent.

Incongruence is the state of a person who is not in a harmonious relationship with himself because of an internal conflict that becomes visible through behavior. It may be (1) sequentially – an action followed by another which contradicts it – or (2) simultaneously – that person declares that he agrees with some- thing, with an uncertain tone.

3 Non-Verbal and Para Verbal Language

Listening does not involve only hearing, interpreting, and providing feedback. Listening involves the use and interpretation of the nonverbal aspects of communication. We transmit messages using words, gestures, voice, and body language. It was found that the impact we have on people in the first minutes is

based 60% on visual messages, 33% on messages transmitted by tone of voice and only 7% on communication content. Although during the interaction, the weight of the content increases, it does not exceed 50% in the impact of the communication.

This somewhat shocking data shows us the importance of nonverbal messages. Nonverbal communication modifies and complements what is to be said. However, many of us are not aware of the nonverbal messages we transmit to others. Even more important to note is that, when there is a discrepancy between verbal and nonverbal signals, people pay more attention to the latter.

Many specialized books suggest that nonverbal messages can be understood and separated from the rest of the communication methods, and that certain signals, such as crossed hands, always signify resistance or lack of interest. Such information can lead us astray. Nonverbal communication always appears in a certain context and is part of a pattern or a habit.

Communication, understood in a broad sense as a trading act inevitably, in situations of interaction, it becomes essential for both personal and social life of the individual. Thus, notions like communication and language have a plurality of meanings.

It is considered that the nonverbal messages we transmit may reveal more than our words. We transmit on nonverbal channels considerable amounts of information. The posture of the body, the gestures, and the tone of voice all reveal a lot of things about our personality, our emotional state, about the safety we have, about the trust we can inspire.

Both your ability to evaluate your client's nonverbal clues and work with them, as well as verbal communication and nonverbal clues coming from you and impacting your client are equally important. Understanding the nonverbal signals of the interlocutor helps you to correctly perceive what it feels like to be on the other end.

Reading the unconscious responses of the body is engrained in our genetic code and it has been working for thousands of years as a radar that protects us and keeps us connected to ourselves and to the environment. There are a number of facial expressions that reveal universally recognized human emotions, and the use of these expressions is more genetically inherited and unconscious than learned and socially programmed.

The six universally recognized facial expressions convey the following emotions: happiness, sadness, fear, loathing, wonder, and mania. The science that handles the study of body language proclaims an undeniable connection between the brain, feelings, thoughts, and bodily movements. In the analysis and interpretation of the body language, the fact that physiological manifestations depend very much on the context of the moment in which they occur, so what you express unconsciously and involuntarily in a situation can mean altogether something else in another context. We must therefore avoid the interpretation of singular signals. For a valid conclusion, several combinations of signals that sustain the overall image, as well as the identification of micro-gestures transmitted by the subconscious: dilation or contraction of pupils, a lift from the eyebrow, should be considered. Movement of the corner of the mouth, all are imperceptible movements for the untrained eye. These can help to accurately assess the emotion be- hind potential false signals. For example, if someone scratches their nose, that doesn't necessarily mean he's hiding something or lying, but he may just have an itch. At the same time, body language is not only subject to cultural and ethnic differences, but also to age and gender.

Communication can generate research, ideas, contradictions, and creation. Nonverbal messages remain open to speculation and deductions and can only make sense in the context of the individual and his relationship with another person.

When you translate the signals of body language into feelings and give them significance, keep in mind that an isolated signal does not necessarily indicate a certain meaning, but that an entire suite of signs is more justified to render significance. An isolated signal is not an indicator you can rely on. Body language is just one of the indicators of why a particular behavior occurs in a situation at some point.

The eyes represent a significant aspect of the nonverbal guides we transmit to others. To a smaller or greater extent, it seems that we all have the ability to read each other's eyes, without knowing how. We simply do it unconsciously. For example, we know when we have visual contact with someone at an appreciable distance, about 30-40 meters or even more; much too far away to see the details of the person's face. Unbelievably, we can see if the other person's eyes are focused towards us and we are able to notice the difference between an empty glance and a fixed look.

Body language means more than just positions and body movements. It includes the way we position the body, the space between us and other people, the proximity and the way it changes, the facial expressions, the eyes, the way they move and focus, the touch, the way we touch ourselves and others. The way our bodies interact with other objects, the way we breathe and other less observable physiological effects, such as heartbeat or sweat. So, the understanding of body language helps us to improve and redefine what our body transmits or says about us, which generates a positive transformation in the way we feel and act.

Visual contact is extremely important in communication. There are, of course, cultural factors that determine to what extent and how often we have to focus our eyes on the speaker, but there are also universally valid aspects. If the lack of visual contact shows nervousness, insecurity or indifference, *excessive* visual contact can be interpreted as if we want to *devour* the interlocutor. These aspects vary depending on the people involved in the communication. In general, eye contact expresses interest and desire to listen.

The voice. The frequency, the tone, the rhythm, the inflections of our voice are extremely revealing. High frequency, fast speech, for example, signifies enthusiasm and excitement. A low, monotonous voice may indicate lack of enthusiasm, weightiness or even depression. Most often, the biggest impact is given not by what we say, but by the way we say it.

The physiology communication

Physiology is an accumulation of bodily characteristics (posture, respiratory frequency, etc.), correlated with a particular psycho-emotional state. Physiology changes both your emotions and your mental representations. For example, if you have a mental representation (a picture in mind) where you see yourself very relaxed, calm and reconciled, but then adopt a physiology (i.e. a position of the body, a respiratory rhythm, etc.) that you have in situations of stress and fear, you will see that the *Will* changes very quickly.

By using the right physiology and by changing the representations we get what we want, which is to change emotions. From emotions we then get to the behavior we want to change. Physiology includes a multitude of things: muscle tension, what you eat, breathing, posture, etc. These things also affect your health. Internal representations and physiology work together, forming a loop or a system that determines your unique personality.

1. Facial expressions

There are authors who assert that many emotions are accompanied by unique expressions of the face, which can be recognized regardless of cultural differences. Facial expressions that signify hatred, joy, loathing, for example, can be easily recognized everywhere in the world. In a working situation, the smile can transmit a condition favorable to a friendly atmosphere and show encouragement and support.

2. Position of hands, arms and legs

The way we sit, the position of our arms, if we keep our legs crossed towards the other person or to one side, all can indicate what intentions we have. If we sit or stand with our body somewhat reversed from the speaker, we express the lack of interest, or that we no longer wish to continue the conversation. Insecurity can be signaled by a hand covering the mouth or gesture of playing with your hair. A lawyer must be aware of his own gestures, as well as those of his client. They say a lot about what will happen.

3. Pauses in speech

For many of us, silence is a source of discomfort. It makes us feel insecure and bothered. However, pauses in speech may mean what we think about what the speaker is saying, that we offer him the opportunity to continue and that we are patient. During a meeting, the lawyer can use the breaks to help the client and observe the body language, eyes, gestures and facial expressions.

Communication Skills

Effective communication skills are vital in the successful practice of being a lawyer. Any attorney needs to communicate well with his clients, colleagues, partners, suppliers and courts. Improving how you communicate will allow you to express yourself more confidently, and more trust means more clients and greater power to convince your opponents and turn them into allies.

Master the art of communication because, in this way, your practice will become a pleasant experience, the clients will appreciate you more and you will enjoy helping them. Your business will become more profitable. You will attract more clients and you will quickly increase the number of paying clients. A well-trained lawyer excels in thorough knowledge of the law and becomes a successful communicator having the following abilities:

A good verbal communication

Do not rely solely on e-mail and written information. Some things are managed more efficiently by phone, and bad news should be transmitted in person. The negotiations proved more successful when they were debated by phone. Face-to- face discussions with a client allow you to lay the foundation for a reliable future relationship. Do not hesitate to call your client when you know for sure that you will not be able to complete the judicial process at the specified time. A competent lawyer treats any situation with honesty, promptness and openness towards his or her client. It is important that in your speech, there are moments of pause, allowing you to listen, to ask questions, to check information and sources, and to reflect on certain topics in order to truly understand your client's problem.

Effective listening

When your client feels really listened to, it creates a framework of trust, empathy and comfort. Most of the time, the lawyer can intuit what the client is about to say and may, therefore, stop listening carefully. Only when you listen carefully to your client you will be able to refer to different levels of communication that will help you deepen information about that case. To improve your listening skills, we make some suggestions:

- Avoid interrupting your client
- Do not provide answers while your client is still speaking
- Do not monopolize the entire dialogue
- Do not make hasty conclusions
- Patiently await the full explanation from your client
- Train yourself to listen to the client's feelings. The art of obedience means knowing how to focus your attention and to use your intuition.

Good advice

Once your clients' trust is earned, they will want to come back to you to be guided. Offer them tips related to the development of their business or other legal issues.

Your objective should be to help your client solve his own problem.

Flexibility

As much as possible, give up on unfounded assumptions. Stay open to the possibility of collecting as much information as possible to help you complete the picture of the client's problem. It is important to have all the data before you decide to help him. To be flexible means to manage to address the client's problem from different perspectives and to find creative solutions.

Curiosity

When we ask questions, we actually communicate the availability and interest we engage in that dialogue. Being curious about your client helps you stay involved and focused on issue. The questions also give you the opportunity to understand in depth what is happening with your client, and this understanding is vital in successfully completing a case. Addressing open questions can facilitate your client's better awareness and clarification of your own situation, so avoid the *why* questions and replace them with *what exactly?* or *how*. An example of a strong question is this: "What do you think of this?" It is important to assist your client by providing your own answers. The originality of his answers might even give you the key to settling.

Value

Since lawyers rate the time spent with a client, it is vital that the time you dedicate to the discussions is valued to the fullest. Make sure that what you communicate has real value to your client, and that you transmit clear, succinct, and easy to understand messages. Determine what results you want to get after a session and what the value of that result is. Then, plan in detail what you are about to say. If possible, practice your speech aloud before the meeting. Take notes if necessary. At the same time, consider the fact that often the meetings do not go as planned, so be well informed and prepared to anticipate and solve the challenges and unforeseen situations.

Persuasion

To be successful, a lawyer has to be a persuasive person. The power of persuasion is important in negotiations when you plead against the courts and when you answer the requests of the clients. To be a persuasive person, you need to be curious and open to new ways of thinking, and beliefs and values that are different from yours. This change of perspective will help you quickly adapt your argument according to these systems. The successful practice as an attorney is based, therefore, on the ability of effective communication skills without which lawyers would not be able to really connect to their clients.

Efficient use of questions

Under the influence of language, perceptions end, and sense and significance enrich and become observable. When evoked with words, the representations are generalized. On a deeper level, in the absence of language, we cannot speak of the formation of notions, judgments and reasoning; it is not possible to type problem- solving activity. Dialogue is used to obtain new information, to exploit possibilities and to trigger actions. The common language of open dialogue shows that both the lawyer and the client are ready to examine and remove their prejudices, unfounded assumptions, hidden personal interests and confusing ways of thinking.

One way to avoid misunderstandings is to ask questions that recover information, clarify meanings and add answer options. Questions have a very strong impact. They cause a search; going through all the ideas, memories and experience of the interlocutor. Questions contain conjectures and axioms, they can open windows to new areas of experience, or they can, as well, close them.

Questions can be:

- Internal – directed towards yourself
- External – directed towards others

- Direct/precise – in search of truth. Direct questions require the speaker to extend or explain in detail the position he adopts:
- Directed – Questions of the type: "Do you find that...?"
- Manipulative – When the one who asks tries to obtain from the one asked a certain answer, which corresponds to your goals
- Closed – questions that close the possibilities of response, because they have two variants of response, *yes* or *no*. Sometimes these questions are needed to bring the conversation back to the topic in discussion, if the per- son guided changes the subject or digresses. In general, however, this kind of question should be avoided.
- Open – Increases the response possibilities and are of the type: "What?", "Why?", "Who?", "When?", "Where?", "How?", "what causes...?" They are questions that encourage the interlocutor to elaborate and reveal his true thoughts, feelings and ideas. They are also useful to stimulate creative thinking and problem solving.

Questions can bring light to a certain place but, at the same time, leave other areas in the dark. In other words, questions direct the client's attention to certain problems, while removing it from others.

Here are some concrete directions for questions to ask your client in their consultation. This will also help to inform you about the case you are asked to solve:

WHAT?
Look for information
Identify objectives

WHO?
Look up information about people

WHY?
Search for justifications and grounds for various human actions

Look for values
Assign culpability
Look for meaning
Search for grounds and past causes

WHEN?
Accommodate in time
Look for information related to a certain moment
Search for signals and trigger mechanisms for actions

WHERE?
Look up information about places

HOW?
Identify means
Obtain information

But how do you figure out the right time to ask a question? Well, choosing the right context for the questions you want to ask your client requires intuition.

Intuition

Intuition represents a person's ability to understand in a fraction of a second, without a prior rational analysis, an apparent phenomenon of previous misunderstandings. Also, through intuition, we understand spontaneously, when one must take an action. Intuition can be practiced by listening and calibrating. Once you become more skilled at listening and calibrating, you will begin to synchronize your questions better, as you will get used to listening beyond words and noticing the nonverbal signals.

Hearing

Active listening means to follow the verbal content, main ideas, and argumentation, but also the nonverbal message, coherent contradictions in argumentation, the structure of the message (pros and cons, advantages and disadvantages), while summarizing the message.

Interactive listening involves the possibility of interacting directly with the speaker on two paths: asking questions and requesting confirmation of the message. Interaction with questions is specifically facilitated by open questions. The interaction with confirmation is based on elements such as: paraphrase (repeating with your own words what you were told), summarizing the message ("so in words..."), and the request for completion ("Can you provide more details about...?").

Relational Rapport

The results of our interactions with each individual are determined by the skill that we manage relationships with, the way we are influenced by them and influence we have over them in our terms of thinking and behavior. So, if you want to be more than a passive bystander, it's very important to develop your ability to influence others. Whether you are a lawyer or a parent, whether you sell, buy, manage, drive, train, counsel, relax or have fun, your degree of success in all these areas is about the ability to influence. It implies the skill to build quickly what we call Relational Rapport.

To create and maintain a strong relationship, it takes a strong rapport, just as a solid foundation sustains a high building. The word *rapport* is a term defining the subtle emotional processes of interaction with other people. It is the name given to the process by which two people relate efficiently. It refers to building trust, harmony and cooperation in relation to others. The key to achieving this rapport is acceptance.

Entering the rapport arena means finding common, familiar elements with others, whether we're talking about places, behaviors or attitudes. The same is apparent from the current language, in expressions such as: *To be on the same wavelength... with someone; To find common ground...; To share the same views; Create a bridge; Harmonize with someone.*

This is about a relationship with significant value. In order to establish a good rapport (mutual sense of empathy, understanding and trust), try to synchronize or mirror your partner's dialogue. The body-level synchronization between two people generates unconscious responses of affirmation and acceptance. This rapport can be seen when two people get along well: they match each other's body positioning and the tone their voices. The rapport in general can be unconscious, but still, if we acknowledge this, we can increase our ability to establish and maintain relationships with other people, whether they are fellow lawyers, courts, friends or family.

Using our own behavior, we can *invite* the other person to join us in a different emotional state. For example, initially we can respond to a nervous client sitting and talking nervously by acting the same way, but when we gradually relax and talk more calmly, so will they. If we match our behavior sufficiently with the client, we obtain a relational rapport and that person will follow, unconsciously, our example of relaxation.

The relational rapport is not a relationship of harmony in ideas. If it persists in time, it will develop into a reliable relationship because it forms naturally and can evolve spontaneously from one stage to another.

The relational rapport implies:

- Respect for each other's beliefs and values;
- Harmonization of behavior: general posture, rhythm of gestures, eye contact, tempo of speech, tone of voice;
- Harmonization of words
- Harmonizing the way of thinking: Re-experience or represent our world using the following senses: sight, hearing, smell, taste, sensation of tact. Experienced internally, in the process of thinking, senses are known as representational systems. We use these representational systems in everything we do: remembrance, planning, learning, imagining problems and solving situations.
- Gaining confidence: For this you have to show, from the beginning, that you have the following essential qualities: authenticity, honesty, competence, frankness, congruence.

To be able to relate to someone, you have to consider at least two things: background and behavior. Depending on the context, it is good to first find the elements of common interest that the two of you have. Most of the time, people start with general and *safe* topics in which they have a high chance of finding common interests. Weather discussions and talking about sports, are some of the obvious topics that remove the initial tension and favor the entry into relational rapport. To get to the behavioral level, all you have to do is match the tonality, the rhythm of the voice and the other points mentioned above and say what you have to say in the same way as your dialogue partner.

The most obvious patterns of behavior that can be matched with those of the interlocutor are:

- **Body position**: whole body, head position and shoulders
- **Tone and rhythm** of the voice
- Repeated **movements**

On the other hand, one could say that communication does not always imply the existence of two distinct individuals, because you can try to communicate with yourself, with your authentic inner being. From this perspective, you can enter the relational rapport with yourself. This rapport is a state of sincerity, an open communication between two or more people, and it is very important to determine the situation in which a specific client is found, as well as how this professional relationship will continue.

The connection, harmonizing and understanding are not techniques. These are ways to be open to the client. The real rapport is much more than copying body posture, although two people who are in relational rapport will mirror each other's way of sitting or standing. You will match your body, your voice, your breath, your gestures, your language and your energy with the other person's.

Real rapport comes from your client's unconditional acceptance. It's not the same as having clients that you like, though, through practice, you'll end up liking most of them. When you accept your client unconditionally. You will become congruent and when you become congruent, you will be in a real relational rapport with them.

Unconditional acceptance means to be curious about your client. You want to know what it is like to put yourself in his place; to accept not only his beautiful habits or admirable traits and values similar to yours, but also the less pleasant qualities that he might have the tendency to conceal or those he prefers not to speak of.

How Do You Create Relational Rapport?

Listen to the rhythm/fluency with which people speak and reproduce it in conversation with them. After a while, you will notice that you start doing this without having to consciously perform it. The goal is to make this become an automatic part of your behavior.

The rhythm/fluency differs considerably from person to person. Some people talk slowly, with breaks to find their words. Others speak very quickly and seem to have no trouble finding their words. If your style of speaking is slower, you may encounter difficulties when trying to pace with a person who speaks very quickly. You will find that your thinking process changes depending on how you change your speech rhythm. As your ability to pace improves, you will find that the ability to intuit what the other person is about to say will improve.

The process that takes place can be described as you managing to adapt so well to the other person's *frequency* (how they talk, how they think, how they behave), that you take on a *Reading of Thoughts* form.

When we talk about relational rapport, we can capture two processes that flow from one another. The first is the *match*, and the second is *guidance*. The guidance occurs as a result of the match, when, by changing the subject or the course of the discussion, the interlocutor follows you precisely because, initially, you fit well enough with him. The key is that this guidance is based on building trust and mutual acceptance. Guidance also involves switching from one emotion- al state to another.

Matching and guiding creates a pleasant synchronization, as in a successful dance. In the dance, the two partners match, harmonize, and drive each other. When you look at them, you think they're floating on the rhythms of music. If one happened to stumble, the other would adapt. This is the situation in which the relational rapport reaches its maximum goal.

The process by which an individual contributes to building a relationship with someone else is called *pacing*. Pacing is the process of equal breathing, posture, movement, tone of voice and tempo of a person in time to develop a relational rapport. By pacing, we adopt someone else's behavior.

When we talk about the relational rapport, we can equate pacing with gestures, facial expressions, and someone's mood, as a way of connecting to a person's present physical state. We observe in connection with the person that methods such as connecting with the world, or a certain way of acting, observing the person's body – posture, breathing – assimilating all of these and sending them back. By doing so, the other will see, as in the mirror, their own condition, the way they are living that moment, and all this will increase the chances that he will see in us a good, suitable interlocutor, someone similar to him.

Does it seem difficult? On the contrary. Once put into practice, you will notice that it is not a very difficult exercise. When you *pace* with someone who feels sad, you do not need to find the reason for his sadness, it is enough to pace with the way he experiences his sadness.

Often, we are tempted to believe that in order to build a relationship with a depressed client, for example, it is necessary to know all about the reasons for his condition, and then to begin to comment on those causes by giving self-righteous speeches about sadness and happiness. Such an attitude is not the basis for building a relational rapport, especially if the other person is not willing to talk about his problems.

Pacing is something much more discreet and functional, by virtue of the fact that it has the quality to penetrate the character, leaving aside the finance.

As we have seen, communication is essential to success in the law profession. Beyond the intrinsic qualities and the intuitive ability to adapt to the requirements and conditions that it needs, we require something extra: a conscious and systematized effort to improve communication skills and the development of professional relationships.

The Role of the Voice in the Persuasive Speech

Let's talk a little bit about voice tone and modulation. The modulation of the voice is achieved by the pressure of the larynx which produces, more or less, acute notes. The volume is due to the pressure of the muscles used in the exhaling to make it penetrate. Instead of raising the volume (which may be unpleasant), it is more appropriate to slow the rhythm of the voice.

Modulation is the first key to voice expressivity. Our stereotyped habit of using a voice with small variations of tone (when we say "tone" we mean the height of the voice stamp, not its expressiveness) brings us into the universe of monotone people, who always use the same tone and, consequently, bore their audience. Through a simple exercise, we can move to an extended voice which is capable of communicating variety and, more importantly, emotion.

Let's think of some phrases. To say them in certain ways and to cause it to be expressive, we ascend and descend the tone of voice according to what we want to communicate. The higher the variation of tone, the more expressive the phrase. In other words, the modulation of the voice is created by the entire musical heights or notes, with which we pronounce each syllable, to give meaning to the phrase. It is also true that, for the same phrase and according to significance, there are several types of possible modulation. It is true that the cadence of the phrase always varies depending on the pitch. If we pronounce the first word of a phrase with a very high tone, to create harmony, we tend to lower it to the next word. Now, if we start with a low tone, we tend to increase it.

Breaks, tempo and rhythm

An optimal exercise to learn to modulate your voice is to speak the phrase in several parts, introducing a series of breaks. Generally, we are aided by the signs of punctuation. When that does not happen, it is good to create an off-the-cuff punctuation or read the phrase as if it had optimal punctuation. You must know that, apart from being a very important exercise to make our voice more expressive, this is also the method of reading that advertising speakers use.

By proper use of the tempo, we are able to have the right speed throughout our entire speech, contributing to the revival of the desired effect in listeners. In particular, the tempo (as in music) corresponds to the rapidity with which we pronounce the words and respect the breaks between them. But this does not mean that the tempo of a reading or a speech should be the same from the beginning to the end. On the contrary, if we manage to use different speeds in the various parts of a text, the reading will definitely be more expressive.

A useful exercise to gain confidence is by using differences in tempo. By using the difference of rhythm, it is possible to use those accents that make the phrase intelligible and expressive. Essentially, the breaks between words and sentences are calibrated to emphasize a certain concept. Generally, in written text, breaks come naturally from commas, but a speech or reading aloud varies depending on the sensitivity of the orator. So, it is not only possible to confer breaks differently from what is written, but sometimes it is downright indispensable, as in the case of reading texts that are accompanied by images.

Let us remember that the wise use of pauses in speech can sometimes make more of an impact than modulating the phrase which might increase the expressiveness of reading. The breaks help us in revealing a concept in which we want to give attention or special relevance. All this leads the audience to a place of constant curiosity, trying to capture the meaning of what is read or spoken.

On the other hand, our voice is a tool with which we can increase consensus in the relationship of the attorney and the client. With the help of effective voice use we can optimize this relationship.

The four phases of the lawyer-client relationship

There are four fundamental steps that characterize the lawyer-client communication relationship, each with specific objectives, achieved by modulating the voice in order to convey the optimum vocal quality in the sequence of phrases. By using the voice, in harmony with the development of the relationship, the lawyer will be able to lead his interlocutor through a course that implies the following:

- Developing a cordial and open relationship
- Hearing and building the lawyer-client relationship
- Explaining the right approach and adherence to the legal strategy
- Stabilization of the relationship on a personal and human level, as well as mutual satisfaction

The cultivation of monotony by using the same effect of the voice generates risks in the lawyer-client relationship. Attorneys can, at times, speak with a *gray voice*. This can make the lawyer seem indifferent towards the emotional problems of their client, which can cause feelings of frustration. When lawyers speak with *black voice*, even if they are deemed competent, he is perceived as dogmatic and "less than human", which gives rise to an unpleasant experience for the client.

The attorney that speaks with a *yellow voice* communicates sympathy and openness, but little empathy and low authority in generating adhesion to strategy. Attorneys that always use *green voice* convey good empathic relationship, but the lawyer is perceived as a little credible from a legal and professional standpoint. Lawyers using *blue voice* transmit cold and serious relationships, with the risk of a low approval of the client to the legal strategy, because he does not feel involved. The attorney with the *red voice* places great emphasis on the enthusiasm of the client, with the risk of gradual deviation from the common objectives when the enthusiasm decreases.

Significant Situations

The situations in which you can develop professional success are the most significant in the life of the lawyer. Here are some contexts that require special attention in the efficient use of communication techniques:

- Relationship with colleagues
- Various aspects of the relationship with the opposite side

- The manner of interacting with the judge, both in the hall and beyond
- The relationship with the magistrate
- Preparation of a text
- A debate in which you want to transmit authority and safety
- Preparing the client before an audience
- Professional telephone calls
- Realization of the economic agreement with the client.

Negotiation Techniques

It has been said that lawyers are the best negotiators. A good negotiator will never give the impression that he wants to convince the other side and to uphold his own interests. In the chapter on communication we talked about relational rapport. The attitude of a good negotiator begins with a different condition that must be built. The relational rapport is designed to build that state which is necessary for a successful negotiation.

Gathering information is fundamental to knowing your negotiating partner. For a Unique Lawyer, a different perspective on negotiation involves considering all aspects of the human being, such as emotions, values, environment, needs, perception, etc. These aspects can either help or destroy negotiations, depending on whether you choose to follow Light or Shadow. Negotiating is like a double-edged sword. You can follow your ego, or you can have an honest, human approach. We talked about light and shadow because we wanted to refer especially to the clarity aspect. Communicate the information that can lead to the solution (light) and avoid the elements that can create confusion (shadow). There is a risk of creating the wrong perception in communicating the message and deviating from the path of solving the problem. This condition can create discomfort and may damage the negotiation relationship.

The negotiation begins by following the awareness of the human side of the negotiating partner. This can be achieved by respecting the needs and interests of the negotiating partner. So, you look like you care about the relationship that the negotiation rapport involves.

Choose a personal approach. Each person is unique and wants to be addressed specifically. A good negotiator knows the human being and understands the needs and goals of each individual. Invite your partner to talk about his needs. Tell him: "I want to understand your world in order to solve the problem."

In general, in the negotiation act, energy is concentrated on combating the other, but a Unique Lawyer will use another set of tools to protect the relationship and solve the problem.

It is fundamental to understand the differences you have in addressing a problem, whether it be about purposes, approach, or solutions. Stay focused on your objective and keep an overall perspective on the whole act of the negotiation. Put yourself in the place of the other party. Empathy is the most powerful tool for a negotiator. Observe the language the speaker uses and try to speak *in his language*. This will create an atmosphere of comfort and confidence, aspects that will facilitate the relationship in negotiations. Take advantage of understanding another point of view. In this way, you can reduce the chances of a personal conflict.

Respect creates the premise of a quality relationship. Do not rely on assumptions regarding the goals of the negotiating partner. Your deduction on the intention of the discussion partner can sometimes be a distorted image of reality, which has been produced from your fears as a result of other similar experiences.

Focus on the present moment, triggering active listening. As stated in the chapter on obedience, it is possible to avoid giving in to your own needs, fears and negative experiences through this kind of obedience. Avoid the risk of not paying attention to an important element, which could be a key to concluding the business or for mediation of the conflict. A good negotiator is always present during the negotiation.

Alina: *I remember negotiating a very important contract once. The atmosphere was very tense. Apparently, both sides encountered difficulties in understanding and accepting the other's perspective. It helped me, however, precisely negotiate within the tense situation, by facilitating presence and understanding of each other's needs. We managed, in this way, to diffuse that loaded atmosphere and we were able to turn a battlefield into a playground, where each had something to gain.*

Stress relief and a positive approach are part of this negotiation game. In our careers as lawyers, we have solved most of the conflicts through transactions. As a lawyer, it is good to understand that concluding a transaction is important for future relationships with your clients. This is a healthy perspective, both for your relationship with clients, as well as for clients themselves.

Establish the standards of negotiation with your client when discussing the settlement of a process through transactions. Assess the cost of time and energy consumed and also losses in litigation cases. From here, start negotiating the fee for concluding the transaction.

It is to be noted that the client's tendency, at this point, will be to direct attention to the time dedicated to the act of negotiation, without looking at the content, the consequences of not ending a transaction. Give up the stereotypical attitude of the classic lawyer! You can achieve better results with a different approach and much less effort.

Another classic lawyer's attitude is the position of attack. You cannot imagine the amount of energy that gets lost when you enter the attack state. This approach affects you, and in time, even your health. Own your instinct to jump into battle if you wish to have good results in the long run. When negotiating partners focus on the "*who is right*" aspect, they will only defend themselves and attack. It's a useless waste of energy.

A good negotiator is relaxed and has control over his emotions. It will turn the perception on the subject of the negotiation. Clarifying the significance of each word describes the intentions of each party. Choose the opportunity to act in agreement with the time and perceptions of the negotiating partner, without creating confusion.

Do not ignore an important aspect which is to consider the values of those involved in the negotiation act. People defend their own principles. Many times, negotiations are difficult because we are attached to beliefs that nourish our ego, and that is a very expensive price eventually.

Analyze what emotions are engaged in during the negotiation. Notice if there is emotion and if so, what kind of emotion is involved (see chapter on Emotions). Try to observe your own emotions and identify whether a certain emotion is related to the moment itself or your negative experiences of the past. Knowing to separate one thing from the other, you will know to channel energy in the direction of achieving the proposed goals, and not in the struggle to master the destabilizing effects of an emotion.

Respect your feelings. Take your time to describe them in your inner dialogue and accept them. In this way, they will resolve themselves. This approach could be a solution to conflict resolution. Start, in relation to the others, from your own perspective. Act proactively, with the negotiator's calm and confident thinking, of the negotiator who knows who he is and knows that he will win, one way or another.

A different mindset can completely change your attitude in front of the interlocutor. We are different human beings with different perspectives. We have the opportunity to act differently from a different place in our inner universe. In the negotiations, emotions come out by reconsidering our ego. The fear of losing hides the need for importance, the desire to find confirmation of your own competence, and the desire for acceptance and the need to validate our role.

Identify self-perception images of ourselves and our self-esteem. Considering personal qualities are very important in the context of negotiations. Sometimes negotiation is used by the negotiator as an opportunity to confirm. Make sure the other side is not in a phase of lack of self-confidence. If this is the reality, adapt your communication by taking this into consideration. All these factors are important and influence the subconscious of the people engaged in the negotiation relationship. Observe the reactions and establish the emotional framework suitable for a productive negotiation for both parties.

If you work with a Unique Lawyer coach, do not hesitate to describe the emotions you're facing. Today, the preconceptions at social levels stipulate that if you show your emotions then you have a weak character, but have you ever wondered where all those repressed emotions were coming from? In the chapters on health and emotions you will find more answers in this regard. Today's world is different from the one we knew. We now have access to tools for balancing and cleaning our inner system to give maximum yield.

When one of the negotiating partners manifests more openness, he can give the tone to the general atmosphere and create another negotiating space and a disdained context. The process acts differently to achieve different results and to strengthen mutual trust necessary for the future relationship of the parties, but also to consolidate your relationship with your client. *Be a Unique Lawyer!*

The frame of negotiation

Create your own positive energy environment. The space in which the negotiation is conducted plays an important role in the process. If you have the opportunity to decide on where the negotiation takes place, then you can choose your space (your office or the conference room of the office, etc.). Now you can start by the way you receive your guests, striving, continuously to make that environment as comfortable as possible.

Cultural Differences

It is also advisable to gather information on the cultural background of the people with whom you interact. A gesture of respect encoded in the language specific to the cultural space from which your interlocutor originates can open common ground much easier than a discussion in universally valid terms. Of course, the opposite can be equally valid: total lack of information or interest in the customs of the adverse party may create a barrier between the parties.

The Voice

The voice also has an important role. We recommend that you use the green voice in negotiation. (See, above, the subchapter about the role of voice in communication.) Also, be careful what you say and when you say it. Find the right time and use the right words. Use the persuasion techniques mentioned in this book.

Time management in the negotiation process

Pay attention to the time factor. It is important that you arrive earlier than the time set for the start of the negotiation. You need time to get used to the space, to acclimate yourself with the other person, to structure your ideas and to show this as a sign of respect for the other side, and also for yourself.

We do not know if you have had to deal with people who are late for important meetings, who are barely pulling their weight, and appear to be descended from another planet. These people arc losing from the start. It is hard to recover such a loss. Some, however, are intentionally late as part of their negotiating strategy to shake the other side. We do not, of course, recommend such practices, but it is good to be watchful so that you can guard yourself when possibly encountering such attitudes. Read more about these issues in the chapter on Efficient Time Management.

Is there a certain label of the negotiation?

Do not neglect your attire. A splash of color might be fine in springtime, but a rigid and serious attire does not constitute a standard in situations of this kind. On the contrary, we believe that attitude and inner state are much more important, and our clothes should suggest this. Not only the way you look can make the difference, but the way you move and how you interact with others at the nonverbal level. Use the Secrets of love: a careful word, a gesture, a smile, are sometimes sufficient to create a quality relationship and a good agreement for both parties.

Negotiation and persuasion

Justice is assumed by negotiation and persuasion. I remember saying that every lawyer has to be a good negotiator. It is a healthy belief that helps us to orient ourselves in relation to clients and the other side. We have to think that everyone has their own objective and follows their own interests. When we know this, we understand what the other side wants to achieve.

But looking out for your own interests does not mean taking advantage of the negotiation exclusively: When we think that what we want for ourselves is the most important thing, we enter into the birth of the spirit of competition which leads to conflict. Intelligent negotiation implies staying anchored in what we want to achieve and considering what the other side wants. When we identify what the other side wants, we can use that to our advantage by giving them what they expect.

Many times, it may be a simple attitude on our part. By expressing this expected behavior, we will remain focused on our goal. It is a method of persuasion that helps the lawyer reach his goal. In college, you do not learn these techniques but, if you read between the lines, you will notice that they are part of the approach of any lawyer who gets what he wants successfully.

Persuasion prerogatives and their importance in the life of a lawyer

It is said that lawyers tend to talk a lot and say nothing. Of course, we try, through this book, but also through our professional activities, to prove that it is just a misconception; an applied label without a profound analysis. Let's not forget that a lawyer must first inspire confidence and for that he must not use empty words. When your words have more substance, you can more easily sustain the trust of others and convince your interlocutor.

One way to relate and gain favor with the interlocutor or the group of people whom you are addressing is to find *a common point* in the discussion you initiate. It starts from a common subject: a need or a desire that anyone may have. It is a way to capture their attention and connect very easily with the person you are addressing. That way, you open the door and you manage to get into someone's space.

If you happen, for example, to go to a client's office or to a colleague's office, lawyer, or mediator, initiate a relational rapport, and find common elements. Perhaps an object from a place you have visited and can make an elegant observation about. A remark about something in the office, or about a fragment that has to do with the speaker which can be a starting bridge for communication. Creating the initial rapport leads the discussion to a point where you can become persuasive.

Persuasive techniques are very precise when we refer to language, words, and tonality. *Words*, for example, matter greatly. How do you use them? How are they used by the interlocutor? Follow along the lines the intent and the meaning that he offers to the discussion and do not get carried away. In general, anything that follows the word "but" has an important value. If you want to disagree with someone, you can use the word "see". In this way, you will direct the discussion to what you are thinking. When you want to draw attention use "So..."

Another useful technique in the art of persuasion is that of *preparing the interlocutor* for what you are about to say. It is a very good technique, especially when you choose to communicate a solution that is unexpected. You can enter an idea into the discussion that was already discussed in a previous conversation. In this way, a sense of familiarity is created, and the new (and unpleasant) information is built on this sense of familiarity.

You can convince them to apply this method: *give credit* to someone to make him accept what you're chasing, accepting your idea.

Use *sensory communication*. Engage your sensory capacities in the direction you want. Create a mentally conducive environment, intensifying the emotions specific to the desired outcome. It is a powerful technique, because our emotions are transmitted and are immediately perceived nonverbally.

Assumptions are often used as a persuasive technique during a conversation. In the context of an account, the alleged issues, that will be accepted by the opposing party are often used inside phrases. Expressions that are supposed to be true in the context of the discussion or in a written communication are introduced. For example: "The price of the house furniture, which is part of the total price, needs to be billed separately." The price of the furniture is assumed to be part of the total price. Or "The Roses in the garden are all red." It is assumed that the garden will be roses.

Other examples of assumptions:

- Time assumption: "While you do that, I will go there." So, you're supposed to be doing something.
- Comments to the interlocutor like: "Normal as...", "lucky you...", "sadly...", "fortunately..." "The good part of this situation is that at least you can get some of the amount you requested, when they could dismiss everything."
- Change the tense of verbs: "You start making the payment, I'll prepare the contract."
- Use assumptions describing how hard it is, how easy it is, how nice, how fast to do something that goes without saying that you will do it "how fast can you change?" "How easy is this for you?"
- The word "or" is strategic in a discussion, when you want to be persuasive. "Do you want to pay cash or credit card?" "Do you want to sign the con- tract now or send it by email?" (You are supposed to have established the signing of the contract).
- Awareness remarks can be successfully inserted into the assumptions used for persuasive purposes. "Do you realize that?" "Do you realize how complicated this is going to be?" "I don't know if you realize you're a priority for me."
- Assumptions that indicate the order: "First, second, last row...", "The first thing you need to understand is how complicated the work is, secondly, the fee will be the measure..."

It uses *positive words*, but especially *positive thinking*. The interlocutor will immediately experience positive emotions. It is important that the interlocutor be relaxed when you want to convince him. You have to capture his attention by asking questions. The questions are their role, depending on how they are addressed. As stated earlier, it can be said that there are several types of questions. There are open questions and closed questions. Open questions allow the interlocutor to give an extended, explanatory answer, and the closed questions make him answer with one word, yes or *no*.

Equally important are the *clarifications* in a dialogue that is intended to follow a particular direction. We all know that clients generally have the talent to divert discussions from their main problem and that can sometimes lead to arguments that very easily can distract you from the main topic. In such cases, the most appropriate thing is to ask for clarifications to obtain quality information to help you solve the problem. For example, ask: *"How specific?" "What exactly do you mean when you say...?" "What exactly is important...?" "Specifically?" "When exactly?" "Who said that?" "How do you know that?"*

Personal issues often occur, allowing indirect questions. For example: *"I was wondering what it would be like if...?" "I was curious as to how it happened...?" "Can you tell me, please, how...?" or "I am interested to know how, when...?"*

Keywords

Be careful, during the discussion, to notice what words your client uses and isolate the words most used, his favorite words. For impact, filter them during conversations and observe his reaction.

Speaking of persuasion, we must acknowledge the boundaries, conjuncture and preparation of the discusser but, first of all, we must respect the ethical objectivities. The most important thing is to identify a person with his persuasion strategy so that you don't get caught up in the analysis that he could carry out on you. In applying these techniques, an experienced interlocutor will immediately perceive that he will not be able to defeat you in this confrontation.

But would you say, the most convincing instrument in a debate should not be the legal basis? Of course, at first glance, that's the way it should be. But if we observe the great lawyers, these businessmen resort to such techniques. These are techniques you don't learn in college. But in the real world, they are so important, and so effective!

Another technique to convince, bizarrely, is precisely that of not wanting to convince.

Andreea: *Personally, I like this technique the best, but I couldn't use it until I had already achieved some years of experience. I was so sure of myself; I didn't need to convince anyone.*

Your level of self-confidence is fundamental to controlling the situation. You cannot be persuasive by arguing unsubstantiated arguments, because you risk being viewed as ridiculous and your credibility will drop in front of the others. In front of the judge or client, self-confidence and the way you expose a problem helps you build your credibility.

Credibility is another important pillar of the image itself. When you are honest, when you put aside any strategy, you express the truth that you're sure of, and people will believe you and thus you will have more to gain.

CHAPTER 4

A healthy lifestyle for a unique lawyer

Do things wholeheartedly!

Carefully.

Bringing the best to all others...

Chapter 4:
A healthy lifestyle for a successful lawyer

Nowadays, we all know that we need to eat vegetables and fruits and exercise regularly to maintain our health. However, this is only the tip of the iceberg. A healthy lifestyle means something more than that. It means organizing your whole life in the spirit of keeping a healthy balance between body, mind, and soul.

We spoke, in the first part of this book, about the necessity of maintaining a balance between your personal and professional life. We believe that this is imperative and should include improving your quality of life and cultivating ways to enjoy life more and to pursue our profession in a different state of mind.

The lifestyle of a Unique Lawyer includes the ability to prevent failure in your personal life. A personal failure can also attract a professional failure. This is a combination of choosing a healthy lifestyle and maintaining the awareness that client problems are not your problems. The lifestyle of a Unique Lawyer involves the discovery and application of some secrets that help you stay lively, energetic and enthusiastic while practicing your profession.

Our experience in the field of personal development and understanding of our own inner profile, made us understand that the profession of attorney can be a chance to grow personally if you know how to interpret the gifts that the various experiences offer you professionally. We have the opportunity to interact almost every day with different clients, and colleagues, so there is a diversity of situations that provoke us to adapt, to think differently, and to apply different strategies, depending on the character of each client and of each individual case.

We experience situations where the client comes to us as their lawyer as he would talk to a priest or a psychologist. For him, the lawyer may be the last possibility to solve his problems. At that point, the professional's ability to remain lucid, to not mix things up, not to take on negative energies or client problems is key. In such situations, you need to apply the art of being empathetic, dosed in a balanced manner. You need empathy to understand your client and you need balance, so you do not take on his problems.

We have seen situations where the lawyer felt guilty that he could not do anything for his client. For example, a colleague felt very guilty about not being able to intervene in a divorce.

The lifestyle of a Unique Lawyer is described by the awareness of this secret of the balance between personal and professional life. One of the most effective ways to protect against challenges often associated with the profession of attorney, but also with aging (cancer, stress, and exhaustion and chronic diseases) is the preservation of this balance.

That is why we developed the *Unique Lawyer System,* in which we show you how to achieve and keep your personal and professional balance. We want this system to be part of the personal education of any successful lawyer. When you enjoy your profession, when you have professional satisfaction, you're full of enthusiasm and, on top of that, you're healthy, you can say you're a successful person. Lawyers who are at the beginning of the road have the opportunity to follow this program and to be counted among the first generations of professionals who apply the principles of a balanced life, following their vocation to a deeper level.

In the chapter "Before Choosing to Become a Lawyer", we talked about the motivations and beliefs that can lead you to choose this profession. In recent years, we have met more and more colleagues who want to give up this profession. If these colleagues had the opportunity to choose their professional route based on similar guidance, their lives would likely be better and more balanced now.

We try, through all the programs we create, to treat root problems, to solve the cause of frustrations in this profession. The mental, emotional, and physical balance gives us the guarantee of practicing the profession in a different way than that in which we were told, not only to ourselves, but to our clients.

When choosing the profession that truly fits you, you can see the difference between yourself and those people who practice this profession with feelings of frustration, guilt and lack of fulfillment.

The profession of attorney is probably one of the few professions in which human consciousness lies on the boundary between truth and untruth, light and darkness, failure and success. From the moment you take off your business suit, you must have the courage to look in the mirror of your own consciousness.

We believe that the successful thirst that characterizes the legal profession still exists in sporting competitions only. It is about a mental competition. It is a profession in which success is expensive, sometimes too expensive and can mean the illness of the soul, the staining of consciousness and subsequently physical illness.

Every profession has its beauty and its risks. The risks are evident in the case of professions that involve a certain type of physical work, even if not seen immediately, and in the case of professions that involve working with people and intellectual work. Law is one of the most stressful professions. It may be the cause of many ailments, such as exhaustion, chronic fatigue, including cancer, ulcers, and insomnia. In a previous chapter, we talked about specialized studies on this subject, published in magazines of prestigious American universities.

The way we perceive and conduct our profession influences our lives. When we have a negative attitude, we facilitate stress and inefficiency, and this affects our entire life. But if we manage to practice our profession with a positive attitude, the solutions are easier, and the professional results are harmonized with personal fulfillment.

Optimum nutrition for a day full of vitality

The way we eat, especially in contemporary society, is a controversial subject, which causes many misunderstandings and confusion. First of all, we would like to remember the simple rules, but also the tough ones of nutrition.

Harsh rules - Tough rules are the ones we keep strictly, daily, to gain lasting vitality. We will offer examples along the way.

Simple rules - Simple rules are useful for acquiring vitality and duration, but you are allowed to deviate sometimes.

The reality is that not all of us are as sensitive (or strong). There are individuals who seem able to abuse their body for years, without noticeable damage. However, sooner or later, all will pay the price of ignoring healthy habits and lacking discipline in choosing a healthy lifestyle. Many of us choose short-term satisfaction because we are not aware of the disasters that we attract in the long run. At the moment, it is a well-known thing that nutrition plays a crucial role in the development of heart disease, vascular diseases, and cancer.

The human being is the only species capable of higher thinking. Unfortunately, there are individuals who use this ability only for their job and business, but not for their own vitality. In the long run, you will have a lot more advantages if you are willing to change a few things and replace short-term pleasures in favor of the quality of life in the long term. We can only offer you advice that we have found that works for us.

Harsh rules

Reduce animal protein: beef, pork and chicken. Try to eliminate or reduce dairy products as much as possible.

Many physicians encourage dairy consumption due to lack of information. For a traditional doctor, taught to prescribe antibiotics and medications that suppress symptoms, there is no logical link between milk and certain foods. There has never been extensive research in this regard.

Milk is bad for everyone, whether we realize it or not. This statement may sound harsh, but it is true. Milk is most harmful when we drink it during meals, because it blocks gastric acid, slowing down and reducing the body's ability to digest. Simply, milk is not good because it contributes to osteoporosis and to the calcification of the arteries. Contrary to what the dairy industry supports, milk decalcifies the bones. It turns out that in countries where milk consumption is high, the percentages of osteoporosis are the highest. We have been so indoctrinated from advertisements over the years that we have come to trust in false claims. "You Will be Stronger with Milk" – here is a false statement. Moreover, the number of people who are lactose intolerant (the enzyme required for the breakdown of milk sugars) has increased. Milk drinkers are prone to indigestion and gas, especially stressed people, so it is better to give them almond milk or rice milk.

Cheese is recommended to be consumed less. Do NOT eat this every day. Cheese is hard to digest and represents a burden for digestion. Yes, we know, cheese is delicious and no, you will not die if you eat cheese once in a while. However, if you consume it every day or very often, you do it at the expense of your vivacity. So, choose a long and dynamic life and don't be like most people who say, "If they can't eat milk or meat, then there's nothing left." That's not true. There are enough options to enjoy. The question is: do you want to feel really good or not? The choice is yours. Choose the quality of life you desire and explore new opportunities. There are plenty of options, gifts that life gives us on the roads we are invited to travel.

Limit your coffee intake. This will make you sad, so we will do everything we can to explain why in detail. Coffee is delicious, but it is the most damaging factor to your energy when you drink it in the morning. That is when your body is still in the process of detoxification. Coffee blocks the body's natural ability to remove toxins. This process begins during the night and continues, for a period, during the morning, which means that the choice to drink coffee in the morning is a mistake. It is advisable not to drink coffee before 11 am, and that you should make sure that you do not drink more than 3-4 cups of coffee a day. If the idea of quitting coffee makes you nervous, drink espresso (the longer you drink it, the more harmful it is). Drink a glass of water after every cup of coffee. Coffee dehydrates. It drains water from the body just like alcohol.

Coffee does not actually offer you energy. Eventually, it will deplete the reserves of your adrenal glands. The adrenal glands are essential pawns in the struggle with stress. When the adrenal glands are depleted you will be more susceptible to suffering from exhaustion and other diseases associated with it. Of course, there are many people who drink coffee and who, apparently, have no problems. Still, it is only a matter of time before they get a warning signal. Sooner or later, they will suffer the consequences of this consumption.

Coffee increases the acidity of the body and can accelerate the road to rheumatism and arthritis. There are various people who say that after drinking a cup of strong coffee or an espresso, they can fall asleep with ease without suffering sleep disorders. This is because of the fact that the adrenal glands are so exhausted, they no longer react to the stimulus of caffeine. It is not a thing to be proud of.

- For optimum vitality you should follow these rules:
- No coffee in the morning, before 11:00 am
- No more than 3-4 cups a day
- No coffee after 7:00 pm, because it influences the effectiveness of your sleep.

So, what can you drink? The best drinks are red tea (rooibos), or mint tea, instead of coffee. You can have a thermos with you at work. We recommend herbal tea, but not the aromatic black tea, real herbal tea. There are hundreds of options in the stores with healthy food and even at the local supermarkets.

Eliminate or reduce sugar as much as possible. Sugar acts at the expense of your body, especially if used in large quantities, and can cause excessive wear and exhaustion. Think about the emergence of certain types of bacteria that produce harmful substances and block the absorption of important nutrients in the intestines. Sugar has similar effects to coffee, giving us a temporary stimulus, followed by a fall. It creates addiction because the body continuously feels the need for sugar and enters a kind of withdrawal in the event of stopping the daily dose. Preferably you should not use sugar at all and replace it with honey (and this in moderate doses).

Remove or reduce refined carbohydrates as much as possible. We find refined carbohydrates in white bread, white rice, white pasta, cakes, ice cream and pastries. Now you are probably asking, what is left for us to eat? We assure you that your taste in food can be taught. You can consume whole wheat or whole grains, such as brown rice, for example. It is seldom possible to order brown rice in restaurants, but you can search for an organic vegetarian restaurant. Instead of white rice, you can consume more vegetables.

Strive to eat as healthy as possible at home, to ensure a good foundation that allows you small excesses from time to time. Whole grain bread or croutons are superior to white bread. They contain more fiber that is good for the intestines, facilitating the elimination of toxins.

Eliminate or reduce animal fats and cooked food as much as possible. The animal and cooked fats are found in margarine, fried fats, sausages and ham. It is preferable to use cold pressed oil, such as extra virgin olive oil, with a few herbs and a splash of lemon. Do not use vinegar often because it does not help you maintain vitality. Use it sparingly. Olive oil is very healthy and helps prevent calcification, while animal fats and foods that are heat prepared, and rep- resent the cause of calcification.

Fried foods are damaging to our body and should be consumed as little as possible. If we eat a portion of French fries every once in a while, it is not a disaster, but if we eat them regularly, they will shorten our lives. And if that is not enough, your quality of life will drop, and you will lose your chance at a long life full of vitality.

Practical Tips. Simple Rules

Breakfast

It is preferable for breakfast to consist of fruit. It is recommended that before eating, you drink a cup of warm water. Fruits directly inject your body with glucose, which gives you energy. Having the same breakfast every day can sound boring. Change offers the taste of life. You can prepare a fruit shake by mixing fresh fruit with almond milk: a fantastic tasty and healthy breakfast.

A good combination for those suffering from hypoglycemia (low blood sugar) is to eat fruit in the morning and then at 10:00 am, have a sandwich to adjust the level of sugar in the blood. It is also preferable to eat fruit in the morning and until the lunch hours. The traditional breakfast consisting of toast and fried eggs is not necessarily harmful, but I do not advise you to do that every day. Breakfast should be easy to digest in order to facilitate the detoxification process of the body.

A heavy morning breakfast drains the body of energy and burdens the digestive system.

Many of us have grown up with the idea that breakfast is the most important meal of the day, so you have to start the day correctly. Nothing could be more untrue. A light breakfast keeps your mind clear and will energize your entire body. Fruit or a healthy sandwich is enough. You will notice very quickly that you will gain more energy. These rules apply to those with a good health condition. If you suffer from any disease, of any kind, it would be wise to consult an expert. There are millions of possibilities related to nutrition and food, and yet there are rules that do not apply to everyone. This would be impossible: we are far too different.

Lunch

The American way of life, promoted so well over the last few decades, has spread across the world: good habits, but also bad. For example, in the business world, meetings take place during lunch. This is disastrous and does not promote a healthy body full of vitality. We work all morning, many of us seated at a desk. It would be preferable to relax by taking a stroll outdoors in the park. So, if you have time, even only 15 minutes, rest or take a nice walk. Ideally it would be good to do a few exercises of stretching and breathing.

What are you eating for lunch? The best option is a tossed salad with olive oil, with fish (in case you are not vegetarian). In the winter months another possibility could be a hot soup of vegetables with whole wheat bread.

Dinner

You can choose the entrée as a green or mixed salad. It is preferable to prepare your salads with cold pressed olive oil (extra virgin). Strive to have dinner by 7:00 pm. The later you eat, the less restful your sleep will be, and the body will have to use more energy to digest the meal.

Dinner can be a hot meal. Consume as many vegetables as possible to improve the elimination of toxins during the night. If you have eaten protein throughout the day, like tuna, then avoid proteins at dinner. Choose a vegetarian meal. Too much protein means a burden for the kidneys and the digestive system; it encourages coronary diseases and reduces vitality. It is preferable to drink herbal tea at night and avoid coffee.

Alcohol

Do not consume alcohol during the day. If you want to drink alcohol, choose red wine for dinner (white wine has fewer antioxidants). Do not consume more than 3 glasses a day and NOT every day. Five days a week should be enough. As a general rule, it is recommended to drink a glass of water after each glass of alcohol. This is because alcohol dehydrates the body.

Snacks

Make sure you always have fruit with you. You will often have to wait in court, so it is a good idea to have a snack at your fingertips. We also advise you to always have fruit with you when you travel. Of course, you will need to carry a big bottle of water with you. The same goes for the office: keep a bowl of fruit and a large bottle of water. You can also opt for unsalted hazelnuts, preferably raw, as well as raisins or other dried fruits. Avoid sweet snacks.

Vitamins – for better vitality

Vitamins are essential for a healthy life. If you wish to continue to enjoy the proper functioning of your own body, for a long period of time, enjoy your work until you retire and, above all, continue to feel good, then you should start investing in the future by taking a good quality vitamin. You may think you do not need vitamins because you feel like you eat healthy. The most recent research on this topic is not read very often.

Due to intensive agriculture and fertilizer and pesticide use, food quality has deteriorated significantly in recent years. Even if our fruits and vegetables are beautiful, they contain less than half of the vitamins they had in the past. Research has discovered oranges without a trace of vitamin C. Therefore, the theory that everything is already in our food can no longer be sustained in reality. Organically grown fruits and vegetables contain more vitamins and minerals and fewer pesticides than those cultivated intensively.

Pollution and Stress

We still have a big problem, represented by the growth of environmental and stress pollutants. That is another reason we need vitamins. It is not only the stress caused by a chaotic lifestyle that is much too demanding, but also about what is called *"electromagnetic stress"* that accelerates the number of free radicals in the body.

Free Radicals

Free radicals are atoms that have in their composition, an extra atom that is easily released. For this reason, it connects with other atoms and spoils our inner equilibrium. These are usually oxygen atoms and can have a destructive effect on blood vessels and tissues in the body. Normally, our body produces special enzymes that attack these free radicals: antioxidants. In a period of 20 to 40 years, due to stress and the use of different types of toxins (agricultural pesticides, exhaust gases, chemical additives in the water, cosmetics, detergents, cigarettes), the number of free radicals in the body increased by 20%.

Biological Age versus Real Age

Free radicals cause premature aging. In other words, the body emits signs of aging long before it should. Someone who is, in real time, 40 years old, can have a biological age of 55 years or even higher. And the opposite may be true: someone who, biologically is 30, can actually be 40 years. The amount of toxins in the body can lead to premature aging. Free radicals destroy everything in their path, causing clogged arteries, worn ligaments, and a slowed endocrine system. This is the perfect terrain for developing cancer cells in the body.

Free radicals cause premature corrosion and aging.

You do not have to be a scientist to realize how important it is to keep free radicals under control and neutralize the toxic effects on the body.

There are 3 ways to do this:

- Stimulate the production of antioxidants in the body
- Try to reduce the intake of substances that produce free radicals
- Increase the intake of antioxidants in the form of fresh fruits and vegetables. The most appropriate would be to add vitamin supplements to this regimen.

Vitamins as Antioxidants

One of the greatest achievements in the field of nutrition is the discovery of certain vitamins that function as antioxidants. Some doctors claim that 100 mg of vitamin C per day is enough for the human body. Actually, that is not the case. It has been scientifically proven that vitamin C is one of the best available antioxidants when taken in high doses. Currently, the human body needs at least 2000 or even 3000 mg of vitamin C per day to counteract the damage caused by stress and free radicals.

The best antioxidants are: Vitamin C, Beta Carotene (Pro-vitamin A), Selenium, Zinc and a number of B vitamins. The most affordable source of antioxidants remains vitamin C tablets. Consider that smokers need more vitamin C than non-smokers. Smoking causes a larger number of free radicals in the body.

Absorption

The main drawback of vitamin intake in the form of tablets is that they pass through the intestines. Some vitamins may not be absorbed because they are related to amino acids. Other tablets may be too harsh to be absorbed and others dissolve before they reach their destination. This is partly caused by the manufacturing process and, partly because of the structural complexity of natural vitamins. Duplicating nature is not an easy goal. Most supplements contain binding agents, fillers and other substances to facilitate easy release of vitamins. The production of quality supplements represents a complex assumption. There are also a number of quality producers. So, we recommend that you carefully research the options and opt for vitamins coming from natural sources. It is not a matter how many vitamins you take, but how much you absorb.

Water as a source of vitality

Water is a key element for maintaining longevity and vitality. As you know, our body is composed of 70% water. Anyone can learn the basic principles for achieving and maintaining perfect health. The main principles are displayed in this chapter.

Andreea: *During the training and coaching program, as a nutritionist, I consider primarily the lifestyle of the lawyer I work with, so that I can help them establish a proper diet. People with deficiency consumed many liquids, but we found that they consisted of, in large part, coffee, tea or beer.*
Clearly, it doesn't matter how much you drink, but especially what you drink: Choose water.

People who do not hydrate enough present the following symptoms:

- Low energy
- Less concentration
- More headaches
- Increased tendency of hypertension
- Need to sleep several hours a day
- Stronger body odor
- A weakened immune system
- Poor function of the hormonal glands
- Dysfunction of the digestive tract
- More skin problems and eczema
- Excessive hair loss
- Increased appetite for sweets
- Menstrual problems (in the case of women)
- Back pain
- More allergies

Adequate water consumption is vital for internal organs. In our times we are exposed on a daily basis, to an alarming level of harmful chemicals such as: pesticides, additives, fine dust, preservatives, plastic, heavy metals, artificial sweeteners, chlorine, fluoride and much more. On average, we are exposed to over 80,000 different chemicals every year. Most of these substances affects us at the expense of our health. The technical revolution is light years ahead of our development. That means we have to act now.

How much water do you need?

As I said before, it does not matter how many liquids you drink, but how much water you drink. Normally, two (2) liters of water a day are enough, unless you have fluid deficiency and you have to recover. You deplete your water levels when you drink other fluids and when you drink less than a litter and a half a day.

Which type of water is the best?

Mineral water is the best. It is clean and natural and contains no toxins. Mineral water contains the beneficial minerals of the earth. We recommend that you purchase bottled water in glass containers.

When should we drink water?

It is preferable to consume water during the entire day, especially until 1:00pm. The body needs at least one (1) liter of water shortly after we wake up in the morning. During this period, our body is still eliminating the toxins we accumulated overnight.

Is it OK to drink water during a meal?

Opinions vary. There are opinions that water consumption during the meal thins enzymes and other digestive juices, preventing proper digestion. Medical studies contradict, however, this theory and consider it acceptable to have one or even two glasses of water during the meal.

Is it necessary to consume mineral water?

Mineral water is superior to tap water, provided that the source is a good quality spring. Unfortunately, not all the mineral water meets the quality standards officially stipulated.

In summary, water is essential to life. The necessary consumption of pure water makes the difference in the quality of your life and your energy level, both at home and in the office. Water is the cheapest remedy for a large number of chronic diseases.

Prevention of the effects caused by the radiation of mobile phones and computers

We live in a digital age, where we surround ourselves with mobile phones, modern computers, wireless networks, high voltage cables and GSM, UMTS or LTE networks. GSM (Global Mobile communications System) is the most popular standard for the world's mobile communications system. UMTS (Universal Mobile Telecommunications System) is one of the mobile communication systems of the 4G generation.

All this produces a potential new stress factor: electromagnetic irradiation. There is no doubt of the extent this irradiation causes damage to the human body. It is certain that all electronic devices produce it. For more information about electromagnetic irradiation and its consequences consult http://niehs.nih.gov/.

UMTS and GSM poles are required to maintain the digital network, allowing use of mobile phones and Internet access; but most likely, they are a real threat to our health. Electronic devices produce harmful radiation. The frequencies produced are inharmonious and, as such, destructive to the human body. Human beings work by virtue of electromagnetic impulses. High frequency irradiation determines the atoms and molecules in the body to vibrate in synch with these frequencies. You can compare this phenomenon with the effects of mobile phones on instruments for aircraft, cardiac pacemakers, and electric wheelchairs. Chronic and prolonged exposure to electromagnetic radiation can lead to numerous diseases.

We are trying to handle this subject with great care and responsibility, given the lack of scientific evidence at present. Researchers found that the radiation produced by mobile phones can hinder peaceful sleep. Electromagnetic waves can cause headaches and depression. To worsen things, the phones radiate infrared and electromagnetic waves in the ear tract.

Of course, the best way not to be affected by this radiation would be to give up mobile phones, computers, and all other electronic devices and move to a cabin as close to nature as possible. It is an unlikely scenario, however, and if we want to enjoy the benefits of a life in a modern society, we must look for ways to protect ourselves. This includes purchasing a protective screen or monitor with low radiation level for your computer and replacing your laptop or notebook to reduce radiation levels in the house. By acting at this point you can prevent long-term harmful effects that you now cannot even imagine.

A healthy mind for a fulfilling life

Maintaining a healthy lifestyle should not only mean caring for your body so that it is full of health and vitality. Our well-being is the result of balance between a body that enjoys vigorous health, and an alert and lucid mind, and a soul that is peaceful and satisfied with its own existence.

Subconscious vs. Conscious

Our mind could be conceived as a space in many dimensions. At least three: conscious, unconscious, subconscious. The conscious represents the higher quality level of organization and manifestation of mental life. The unconscious represents the primary level of the organization of the psyche that is structured on the basis of the inborn biological needs and the spontaneous mechanisms of their satisfaction. The unconscious occupies an intermediate place, subconsciously and consciously. Psychoanalysis contributed decisively to the conceptualization of the term of subconscious, which is seen as a kind of anteroom in which he gathered and waited to enter the sphere of consciousness activated elements unconscious.

We can think of the conscious as the top of an iceberg. It occupies between 10 and 12.5% of the total area. Most of the iceberg is hidden under water, just as the subconscious is. Imagine what will happen when the subconscious is not aware of the decisions made by the conscious mind. But let's look to the tip of the iceberg: Here lies the conscious mind, the place where the will is found!

Willpower

The will, in an individual dimension, is a form of conscious and intentional thinking, with the role of self-tuning. Consciously, you might decide to do something specific, but that's not a guarantee that you are going to do that. For example, I plan to get up an hour early to exercise, but the act itself to go to the gym depends on my mood. My subconscious will always try to convince me to spend an extra hour in bed, convincing me that this is so much better for me than going to exercise.

Subconscious

The subconscious is that part of the mind that has control. All your memories, about everything you have lived, seen, heard, felt, are stored here. Consciously, we do not have access to this storage space where we are also hosted and our feelings. What do you feel when you think of a confrontation situation? What are you telling yourself? What images do you see with your mind's eye?

Emotions

Emotions are maintained as long as there are one or more stimuli to act upon and then they stop when the stimulus disappears. Emotions remain stored in our memory and are reactivated whenever the right stimulus appears. The subconscious houses our emotions and generates them randomly. However, you have the opportunity to control the response of these emotions. Many of us forget that emotions can be transformed using our conscious mind. For example, when you wake up in the morning, it is up to you to transform your mood in a few moments, depending on how trained you are in this process.

Habits

Habits are locked in our subconscious. Synaptic nodes preserve the usual patterns. We'll give you an example. A 3-year-old does not know he cannot swim. This fact is named consciously incompetent. Later, the child takes swimming lessons and moves easily to the consciously competent stage. Now he knows how to swim, but he has to focus on the moves. Then he can become a fan of swimming and he can enroll, for example, in water polo. He no longer has to focus on the swimming act.

Now he has gotten to the point where he is competently subconscious. It has passed through the learning cycle, from incompetent subconsciously and has reached the competent subconscious, thus developing an "automatic pilot" for swimming. Remember the moment you learned how to drive. Remember your first lesson as an aspiring driver? How impossible it seemed to have to think and perform so many maneuvers simultaneously.

Once it has become a habit, any gesture is fixed in our system, where it becomes increasingly difficult to make changes.

Imagination

Our subconscious also contains an ever-surprising dimension: that of imagination. The act of imagining a clear and natural picture has an instantaneous effect on our mood. Imagine you are biting a slice of lemon. Taste it, feel it and see it clearly. The only thought this action gives is the reaction of your taste buds. When we wake up after a nightmare, our body is usually wet because of sweat. Here is a clear reaction of the organism to a stimulus that is not found in our immediate reality.

But the incredible power of our imagination means more than that. It means that you can use your imagination to give birth to new ideas to make your life easier and to create the change you want to see in your life, both in your personal and career plan.

Our subconscious protects us

This happens in two different ways. One of the strategies is called *Critical Thinking*. It is that skeptical part of the subconscious that is cynical and full of judgment. The critical mind stands between the conscious and unconscious as a goalkeeper. It happens quickly to reject certain concepts because of disappointment. When we were kids, we believed in many things that turned out to be not true such as Santa Claus, fairy tales, elves and fairies. At some point, I realized that all those lies had actually helped us to develop critical thinking; to protect us from absurdities or disappointments.

Our brain is the most active when we are in a waking state (when it activates critical and rational thinking). When we're relaxed, the alpha waves in the brain are getting bigger, the critical thinking goes into the second plane, giving the creative subconscious the opportunity to assert itself.

The other strategy is useful for protecting us from physical and emotional pain, and suffering in general. The subconscious hides or erases memories that we find too painful to remember. Life continues and the subconscious blocks any connection with painful incidents that it recognizes as possible threats of what has happened in the past. When we want to make changes in our lives, it is very important to involve the subconscious and make it understand that this *protection* no longer works – and that it has actually become an obstacle.

The subconscious must be convinced that its strategies are no longer serving us. That change is necessary, and it is better to cooperate with the conscious. The subconscious knows, however, your best interests. What we want is to ask for synergy: aligning consciousness with our subconscious to acquire the desired results. When we believe that something is possible, both at the conscious and subconscious level, we enjoy a state of fact that we can call *matching identity*.

All these aspects of the psyche, as a mechanism of thought, seem to be natural physiological processes that work automatically, like the hardware of a computer. But it is not quite so, because today even the smartphone you use needs to be adapted with new technology periodically.

How do you adapt your psychic hard drive? We alone are responsible for cleaning our psyches and washing, from time to time, the mechanisms of thought. We believe that the *Unique Lawyer System* is a good start in this respect.

Introducing spirituality into our work

First, let's define spirituality in the context of vitality, labor and joyful life. Spirituality means everything. Satisfaction in work means spirituality at maximum rates. The way you experience life determines whether or not you are on the spiritual path.

Spirituality is not a cumbersome concept, but a natural learning process from your own experiences. This process will make you wiser, more patient, more loving and much happier. It will help you find meaning in your own existence, discovering and developing qualities, abilities or talents that are inside you. If everyday life makes you bitter, angry and frustrated, this reveals that you are not on a spiritual path, but on a path in which you have much to learn. This can make you sick and can rush the aging process.

Spirituality means to discover that there, somewhere, exists more than a physical form of the perceptible universe and that you do not just represent your body or your thoughts and emotions. Spirituality means knowing that your purpose in life is not just to accumulate material things, to be successful, to be better than others, to be famous, to have power, to know more than others, or to have a high IQ.

What is your purpose in life? Here is a good question that can have many answers. In our vision, we are here to learn some lessons about our inner strength (connecting to a much larger EU). We are given the chance to learn that everything in life is like a boomerang: what you offer – you will receive. Being selfish doesn't lead to anything good in the long run. That is why we believe it would be beneficial to transform ourselves into people who believe in power that is undeniably for the better, no matter how much evil happens around them. In this way we develop extraordinary potential and capacities (intuition, etc.), healing internal injuries and releasing negativity to become emotionally and serenely stable.

Here are some lessons of life that would be great for us to learn:

- Live in harmony and love
- Helping our neighbor is often a small gesture that can help us
- We must love ourselves to be able to understand and love others
- Leave the past behind and learn to forgive, both yourself and others
- We will never truly be happy if we remain anchored to the past, in the role of the victim
- Happiness means choosing and that everything that keeps us down can be released without having to repress something
- Vulnerability means power
- Accept that our parents did the best they could, based on what they knew at the time
- All people are equal, despite their race, religion, sex, past or beliefs

- Good will always defeat evil and that your contribution matters to maintain a balance in favor of good

All this applies to your profession because, in the case of many of us, it occupies most of our time. What happens at your place of work and how you react defines you? If you remain in the shadows because you are afraid to be a Unique Lawyer and you are afraid that you will be judged, that you will lose your job, then you sell yourself too cheaply and you will never be happy, rich or full of potential. If you think there is something better for you somewhere if you lose your job or your clients, then it is time to act.

Your skills regarding socialization show you where you are on the scale of evolution. That does not mean that a particular person is superior to another, but that some of us can become more aware than others about their place in the world, their potential and the methods by which they can make a difference. A Unique Lawyer is a professional who has realized his unique role in the career realm he has chosen.

Sometimes people do not recognize all of these characteristics as spirituality because they are naturally part of their being (we call this *natural craftsmanship*). Others see spirituality as a form of naivety, especially those who believe, to a greater or lesser extent that they are superior to others. They must realize that their ego may be tied to their achievements.

How do you gain spirituality? You probably have wanted to attain at some point, both professionally and personally, a point of wisdom. Spiritually speaking, it means to feel, to believe, to have intuition, to free yourself from pain, to stand up and try again. It does not matter how much you have accumulated, but how much you have learned. There are many situations in a professional context where those who are keen to learn can learn valuable lessons. Often, the situations we encounter test us to see if we are able to figure out whether we operate through the power of ego or our inner strength. We must know that the power of ego is built on the basis of unresolved problems and past pain.

Your emotional universe

We can agree that we all perceive the world in the context of our present condition. This is able to explain why we have different perceptions at different times. Considering that we always operate from inside an emotional state – whatever it is – that condition will create and filter the way we process things. You may have noticed that when we feel energetic, we perceive the world differently from the moments in which we feel tired or sick.

Our physiology changes the way we represent ourselves, and how we understand and live in this world. In this way, our inner world always affects the outside world. Thus, our internal representations describe how we live through certain events. I do not necessarily describe what happened objectively but describe a personalized version of how the event was experienced.

Our emotional moods have a strong and comprehensive influence on our thinking and behavior. After identifying and calibrating these states, we invite you to establish how you can use them to enrich your current resources. A way to make them available at any time and to stabilize them at the appropriate moment is necessary.

Equally important is the ability to access a particular state. The actor must be able to get out of the role at the fall of the curtain. In the business world, many people become very motivated to get great things, but after a while they end up getting tired, they destroy their family life, they become unhappy, and in extreme cases, they lose their health.

The management of our inner life requires balance and wisdom. Each of us has a personal history, rich in various emotional states. To repudiate them, we need a trigger mechanism; some of the present associations capable of reliving our initial experience. Our mind makes connections between our different experiences naturally. In this way, we attribute our meaning to our actions. Sometimes these associations are very pleasant. For example, a favorite song can awaken a pleasant memory.

Our state of mind, at one point, is the result of our physiology, our thinking and our emotions. But it is far more than the sum of the parts that produce it. In their dynamics, our emotions and impulses reflect the immediate and direct part of our experience. They vary in intensity, in duration and familiarity. The gentler the emotional state, the easier it is to think rationally. The more violent or intense it becomes, the more the process is shaken and, as a result, you will generate more emotional energy. Our impulses always present an emotional component.

Although we often believe that the emotional moods, we experience are caused by events that get out of control, we actually create them. Any activity you have to accomplish, whatever you want to learn, any objective you propose, ask yourself first: "In what state would it be good to find myself to make this easier?"

Have you ever gotten angry without having a real reason? To get mad at an employee or a colleague without him being guilty? When you have collaborators and are involved in solving a matter it is not just up to you, it is the lawyer's duty to work with the person. Did you happen to ruin a collaborative report without there being a serious reason on your part or from the other one, to have to rewrite a single word or an answer that, at that moment, did not please you? Those situations in which you are emotionally unbalanced can even destroy your collaborative relationship with another person.

Is this about you or was it about the other person? There were emotions that were affecting you, giving you a state of discomfort, which has taken the focus off of you solving a problem, from the conclusion of a transaction or from carrying out a warrant.

There are emotions that we face every day, especially when we are forced to have a collaborative relationship with the other side for a common client. There may be situations where things get so bad that you forget the cause for which you are fighting and you can let yourself be affected by your personal side, your emotions, which may have nothing to do with the issue itself or the purpose for which you are there. You wake up as though you have been trained in a fight that has become personal, though it is not yours.

Emotions can make you lose your temper. It can remove you from the essence of the problem you are trying to solve. Emotions can make you lose your lucidity and cause you to make the wrong decisions. We don't want to say, through all of this, that emotions are sometimes harmful. On the contrary, when we manage our emotions effectively, they can even become the key to our success. Why? Because emotions are part of the authenticity of each person, and authenticity is one of the most important pillars in the scale of the values of a successful lawyer.

Emotions must be expressed in the most advantageous manner for us, but also for others. Repressing emotions causes you to have inappropriate reactions and have a negative status throughout the day. So, our emotions are a great gift, but they depend on our ability to use them, so as to give us the energy to overcome any challenge. Each has its own unique gift. It depends on how we use them, whether we are the creators of our lives or the slaves of our own emotions.

Managing negative emotions

The techniques that we are going to present are tailored to the legal profession and we want our colleagues to become aware of their own resources and, at the same time, to understand how they can use them from a unique perspective. Because each of us is unique and we are beings with unique resources and gifts.

There is, of course, also in our field professional ethics that we all should commit to respect when we embrace this career. We believe that a Unique Lawyer will learn to listen to other principles, present at the level of personal consciousness.

The techniques are simple and easy to follow. We are guiding you according to the theory that every action today brings tomorrow's results.

Examples of negative emotions:

- Frustration, Annoyance, Anger, Hunger, Envy
- Guilt/Sense of guilt Care/Concern
- Fear of failure
- Fear of being Judged Jealousy
- Tension

Examples of positive emotions:

- Joy
- Sense of security Calm
- Inner peace/Inner balance
- Enthusiasm
- Courage
- Optimism
- Generosity
- Serenity

As you can see from the above lists, negative emotions always have a positive correspondent. Besides the negative or positive emotions that we express, we are subjected to complex general behavior, which creates a certain image in the eyes of others.

Our emotions are accompanied by a series of reactions that, over time, form our habits and subconscious mental patterns, which we apply to a certain situation in our career similar to one of the pasts. Therefore, we must acknowledge the nature of the emotions that dominate us at some point and be attentive to their implications in our behavior and in our mental state, but especially the way we react when we are surprised by a certain emotion – negative or positive.

For example, when you acknowledge that you are in a situation where you have a feeling of fear, the first thing you have to do, after you have identified the feeling, is to start a positive dialogue with yourself. Remember that every negative emotion has, as a reverse, a positive emotion. The emotion opposite fear is courage. At this point it is recommended to focus on courage, on the opposite emotion.

Negative Emotion: Fear

Facial expression: eyes wide open, tense face, immobility.

Verbal expression: blockage in expression, knots in the neck, weak voice, insecurity.

Tone of voice: slow, low voice, unperceived.

Actions: inability to react.

Behavior: blockage in behavior, insecurity, disconcertedness, the need to flee.

Posture: rigid, stuck, steady, tense.

How You Breathe: respiratory blockage, uncontrolled breathing, lack of oxygen, short breath, suppression of air.

Thoughts: negative thoughts, panic, lack of solutions, darkening, pessimism.

Mental associations: associations with negative situations, associations with examples, personal or negative.

Mental images: dark, opaque, disastrous negative images that create pain.

Image colors: dark, obscure, opaque.

Image size: large negative images.

Beliefs: fear of failure, fear of solving a specific situation.

Positive Emotion: Courage

Facial expression: open, serene, inspiring self-confidence.

Verbal expression: capacity of free expression, firm voice, safety, fluidity in expression, safety in the use of words.

Tone of voice: emphatic, clear, sure, decided.

Actions: free movement and safe actions.

Behavior: safe behavior, feeling of freedom of movement, firmness, safety.

Posture: mobility, lightness, free and fluent movements.

How you breathe relaxed, comfortable, calm and quiet breathing.

Thoughts: positive thoughts, short-term solutions, long-term solutions, flexibility, skill in thinking, optimism.

Mental associations: associations with beautiful memories, with successful memories, positive external examples.

Mental images: open, light, images that create pleasure, safety, optimism, suc- cess.

Image colors: bright, strong, open, very clear.

Image size: great positive images.

Beliefs: safety will succeed in any situation.

Techniques for managing negative emotions

- Breathing
- Movement
- Viewing success
- Positive affirmations
- Meditation
- The environment
- Posture
- Alkaline/Hydration
- Power of mind/focus
- Rest

Often, in your profession, you fall prey to strong emotions. You feel them all over your body. It is like your heart comes out of your chest in front of the judge, an audience or a meeting with more participants. You may have experienced moments where your breath becomes weaker and you feel like you're losing control of your emotions. But things don't always have to stay that way, especially in the case of an experienced lawyer.

Our emotions can be controlled through training. As we train at a gym for performing physical activity, a successful lawyer can also train themselves emotionally. All of life is a rehearsal, but we choose whether we make it conscious or if it takes us by surprise.

Let's say, however, that you are surprised (unprepared) by an assault of emotions. If you feel your blood pressure rising, you have uncontrollable reactions by a new situation, in a meeting with a new client or in front of a judge and you feel that you cannot manage all these emotions that wash over you, the simplest technique and the most effective at that moment is to focus on your own breath. Focus on the abdominal side. Simply visualize how you inhale and exhale. Realize your breathing must be very slow and keep this pace if you can. This is an off the cuff solution that brings you out of any deadlock. Breathing must be done through the nose. Try to disconnect, for a few minutes, from the outside environment to calm down. This is a very simple exercise, designed to help you manage certain emotions that can make you lose your concentration and strength at some point. But this technique is just one of ten techniques for managing emotions in the profession of attorney.

We must consider the fact that a strong emotional structure helps us to be safer, helps us overcome a difficult situation with more self-confidence, but also to gain, in terms of respect, in front of a client. It is possible to be successful without knowing certain techniques or acknowledging what emotions are affecting you in one moment or another. That is why we think there is a big difference between "success" and "being successful".

To be successful means to be reconciled with yourself, to feel calm and to know how to get out from a deadlock consciously, without feeling frustrated or to regain certain emotions. There are lawyers who are successful but who, at the end of their career, have to spend all their money on doctors because they won't take time out for themselves, their children, or family.

Any decision made in a state of calm is a much wiser decision than a decision made in a state of tension. It is best to wait to calm down and then give your answer or solution to a certain problem. Here, patience is very important. There are times when valuable information loses its value, because you had no patience to give it at the right time.

It is very important that you use the moment in which you communicate something or answer a question. The moment you hesitate, when you are nervous or anxious, you lose the ability to listen to the other person and this may be to your disadvantage. A Unique Lawyer is the one who has the patience to listen to the end, the one who knows that information is of value or not, by the value he gives himself at the time of communication.

Stress

For starters, we have to define what stress means. Stress is not caused by the amount of effort we make or the busy schedule. It is not caused by an unfriendly boss. Some people's stress is saving others. A person who has millions of dollars can be relaxed or stressed. Some people would rather die on the spot than talk in public, while others live to be in the spotlight. It is not caused by external factors, but by our inner response to these factors.

Stress does not mean what happens to you, it is the way you react to what is happening to you. Stress is a state of imbalance, of dysfunction, of inner restlessness and even anguish.

Understanding this concept puts things in a fair perspective. It is irrelevant whether your friends or colleagues are friendly or not. It is irrelevant how many more hours you work overtime or how much work you have to catch up on. It is all about understanding your inner feelings. Your inner dialogue weighs more than any other person could tell you.

According to Zen philosophy, the key to happiness is to be totally present, in the *now*. When we listen to a client, we are aware of every word he says, the way he speaks to us and his condition. When we eat, we are completely aware of how we taste the flavors, feel the textures, the process of chewing, swallowing and the way we perceive food in the stomach. There should be no distracting factors (reading emails, sending messages, discussions, etc.).

Any activity should seize our senses completely. Every thought that distracts our attention should be released the moment it appears. Transform any activity you perform in a five-dimensional experience. This attitude creates space and calm in your life, eliminating stress and boredom. Zen means to always be present, in full, in the actions you are performing.

Andreea: *Recently, I had a conversation with a dear friend about the state of dissatisfaction that the job created. He had come to consider his work boring and tiring and was ready to give up his lawyer profession, he was already looking for another job. Consequently, the current job suffered. I advised my friend to stay focused on the current job for a while. I advised him to perform his duties properly and to arrive every morning at the workplace motivated and ready to respond to his clients' expectations. As I have told him, it is important to realize that we are partially responsible for the best solution of our client's problems.*

The key to enjoying ourselves more in our profession is to put ourselves in the place of our clients. In the *Unique Lawyer System*, we have devised a module that refers to this: *Be your client*. What would you do if you were your own client? Would you give more energy to fulfilment tasks? Would you know when to stop for a while? This module can have remarkable results when the lawyer understands a subtle aspect of the problem. That the best method is to keep a balance between the ability of empathy (knowing how to put yourself in your client's place) and the ability to maintain the continuity of your own identity (staying permanently connected with yourself, with your needs, values and aspirations). Therefore, with the manifestation of empathy, we advise you not to lose sight of yourself in this whole process. You should always take care of yourself to prevent physical and mental exhaustion. This for your own good, but also your clients.

Most lawyers have a difficult time accepting that people who take care of themselves and communicate their boundaries clearly are more precious than those who overburden themselves to exhaustion for the sake of clients who often abuse this availability. All those who suffer from exhaustion *have bitten off more than they could chew*. They failed to create healthy relational relationships with those around them and to delineate their own space and create healthy boundaries.

Creating personal space means knowing how much you can carry and how much is enough. It's no use taking another bite, when you've already bitten off more than you could chew. Enough is enough!

When you need to recharge your batteries, make sure you can handle it. When you need to say no to a colleague or a superior, simply do it. That is all you can do, no more, no less. If you gave the best while you were paid to work, there's nothing else you can do extra. You have to learn to accept this.

The last and most important aspect, when it comes to tension in the workplace, is to learn to understand the feelings and emotions you face. You can only achieve this by working on improving yourself, possibly assisted by a coach, therapist or workshops. Because we are, all of us, unique and different, we need personalized help. There are no universal recipes. We dearly explain this to our students, who ask for our help in workshops that we organize in a safe framework, where they work and face their own emotions, with their own negativity and the effects of stress, to build a healthier life and gain personal fulfillment.

Our coaching courses address both groups and individuals in personalized sessions. You can learn to be happy with yourself, in punctuality you are currently in your life. You can learn how to get more out of your personal relationships and above all, how to get more real satisfaction in your profession life and enjoy life to the fullest.

Our life is composed of a series of incidents, events and moments that define us. How do you treat yourself and others when things do not happen the way you want? How do you respond to rejection? How do you deal with people who show you little respect or none at all? How do you deal with people with negative temperaments or clients who do not know how to treat people and treat you like you are their slave? At what point are you guided by the opinions, views, emotions and actions of others? How do you relate to partners stuck in the role of the victim and asking for your attention on a continuous basis? And perhaps most important: how much tolerance can you grant? What do you accept and reject? When do you communicate your boundaries and when do you fail to do it? Everything is resolved around a central theme: How do you answer life's questions?

Stress and its harmful effects on our lives

Stress has an aggravating effect on various ailments that affect our psyche and sometimes even our soul. More and more active professional people complain of problems with their backs. A massage can play a preventive role here.

Andreea: *Besides the fact that I've known many colleagues who have back problems, I can confess my own experience with back pain. I remember a period of years in which I went from doctor to doctor to find out what was happening to my body, tormented by some insufferable back pain. Apparently, there were not physical causes, but psychically I had gained a lot of tension and stress in the back area.*

Regular massages are essential for maintaining a state of vitality. Masseurs can perform therapy even at the workplace. There are special chairs that offer you a fantastic revitalizing massage. It is essential to discover the exact needs of your body to maintain its balance and act accordingly. Physical exercise (combined with a massage) is fundamental to recharge you vigorously. Of course, equally important are healthy nutrition as well as an adequate intake of vitamins and water consumption adapted to our own needs. We have discussed these issues extensively in previous chapters.

Identifying the reasons for stress in our lives is absolutely necessary to eliminate it. If you value your life, we advise you to develop a habit of writing down your thoughts in a journal. This practice will give you an overview and will help you minimize the influence of this harmful factor.

The five most common reasons for stress

Stress does not suddenly occur in our lives. It has a history behind it. Its effects are only visible when the problem is already present and when our body, after having fought vigorously, can no longer cope with the challenges. We need to look carefully at our daily lives and routines, to detect those habits or tendencies that we sabotage ourselves with, sometimes without realizing it.

Here are some saboteurs:

There are no goals set -- Lack of goals leads to disorientation, waste of time and lack of energy. Maybe it has happened to you that on certain days, you might suffer from exhaustion even though you feel like you have done nothing. Here is the secret: when you don't have a clear goal, you can't measure the outcome. Get used to making lists of long and short-term goals.

Distraction -- These days, information is so invasive that it's getting harder to stay focused on important things. Often, in those short breaks from work that we recommend, there is a tendency to go on different social media networks or search for various information in the online environment. We are not talking, under any circumstances, about this way of taking a break. Not only can these habits distract you from what you have to do, but you can also get tired. The mind needs a break for refocusing. Give yourself this privilege and dedicate a few moments to relaxation that will charge your batteries to retrieve your concentration and the energy you need. All it takes is a moment of distraction, and it will take a long time to enter the state of maximum efficiency.

Lack of knowledge -- You cannot have extraordinary expectations without an extraordinary investment. We do not mean financial investments. Money is only a resource and if you do not know how to manage it, it will lose that quality. We mean the investment in yourself. It is the most valuable investment. Although we have seen many situations where unprepared lawyers were not affected by stress at all because of their own incompetence, we believe that when you engage in a relational rapport and know that you represent the legal rights of a client, you must be ready to support that cause. The need for legal knowledge is, in our case, like oxygen.

How can you control a situation if you do not have the necessary knowledge? Besides being put into a ridiculous situation, inside you will eventually experience a lack of self-esteem. Do not neglect this issue, perhaps it is the most important one for a lawyer. It is important to have the courage to say "no" to situations you cannot control. Recommend someone else or turn to a colleague for help so you do not get caught unprepared by a case you cannot control due to lack of knowledge.

"I want the result now!" -- Lack of patience can trigger a pressure that can create blockages prevent progress, even though you want to do everything very quickly. We went through this situation, but patience helped us overcome the moment. It is important to stay focused on what you have proposed, but at the same time, to detach yourself from an anxious will that blocks you from achieving the objective. It also requires a strong motivation, ready to answer your needs in achieving the objectives, but also of patience. Anxious people are more exposed to heart disease. Deadline pressure can create a strong state of stress, the source of many ailments of the human organism. The desire to accelerate the result also affects your actions, not just the result. Learn to take care of yourself before anything

Lack of self-knowledge -- You may have faced moods you cannot define. In more serious cases, the first step is to go to the doctor and get a diagnosis that gives you the necessary psychic comfort. Avoid medicine as much as possible. Every moment of our lives is different. We are the result of a perpetual transformation. Our body is exposed to continuous interior changes and we must not be afraid of the transition from one state to another. Learn to observe your body and respect it.

Each person owes it to himself know his own rhythm and respect himself. If necessary, bring it to the attention of the people on the team you work with. We have encountered this problem very often on our team. We used to have a very fast and kind of inhumane rhythm. We were able to talk on the phone, listen to what another lawyer says, read email, and give an answer at the same time. This kind of leader or contributor is very stressful to those around him. Unfortunately, it is a person who is very far away from themselves and those around them. When you learn to value your own rhythm, you value that of others. It is for this reason that we insist that you first get to know yourself, so that you can also help those around you.

We will share some tips that can help you face stress more effectively. The first step is to become aware of the tensions and sensations in your body. Most people have no idea what happens to them when it comes to dealing with tensions in the body. It is important to learn how to get rid of tension, because it can accumulate in the body and can create discomfort and can even cause the emergence of various ailments. Releasing and transforming tension prevents it from accumulating in the body and will provide you with a feeling of wellbeing.

Exercise for Stress Release

Step 1: Feel your body and try to become aware of stress, tension and discomfort.

Step 2: Where exactly do you feel the accumulation of these sensations in your system? Mentally concentrate on these areas.

Step 3: Experience and receive without opposing or judging.

Step 4: Inhale and exhale calmly and deeply, while feeling the tension. Relax in this tension.

Step 5: Release tension and accumulated stress.

The release process consists of three (3) questions and one action:

- Would I like to get rid of this tension? There are situations where a certain type of tension motivates the necessary actions.
- Can I relieve myself of this tension?
- When do I want to relieve myself of this tension?
- The most logical moment is now.
- Exercise when you feel ready.

It is time to perform the process that helps you free yourself of any tension present in your body, completely. The best results are obtained when combining the action with visualization and breathing. Choose a picture that is easy for you to visualize clearly. Examples could be emptying a bucket of water that is full to the brim or opening a faucet in a water tank. Until the release, inhale deeply and during release, exhale until you feel your lungs are empty. Repeat the visualization and breathe until you feel that all the tension is gone.

This exercise has many benefits and can be perfected with practice. You will improve each time you do it. At some point, it will become an automatic response when the tension comes up. The reason for increased tension is irrelevant, you will learn to focus only on releasing it. Whatever is out of control is irrelevant. It may seem very simple, but I guarantee you it is one of the best ways to reduce stress, to become more vital and healthier. Moreover, exercise speeds up your awareness process, so you will pay more attention to the effects that others have on you and you will know how to deal with them.

Relaxation exercises with immediate effect

In the previous paragraphs you read about stress, about what it is and how it can be released. Stress is the inability to relieve yourself of tension. Causal factors are irrelevant. Stress can be caused by many things: when you make a mistake, when you have an aggressive client, when you feel unjustified by a judge's solution, when your superiors delegate everything to you, when it is bad weather, when something bad happens at home, when you have to do seven days of work in two days, death of someone you love, dismissal or when you hear bad news. Tension is tension. It has a detrimental effect on your body, your hormones and your immune system. Tension comes with the price of your vital energy and con tributes to premature aging.

Aging, in itself, is not a problem, but the early appearance of signs, with unwanted effects is. Stress, with its untreated consequences, can lead to this. We have previously shared many ways in which you can reduce the tension and stress from your life. The better you become at relieving yourself of stress, the less it will affect you and you will have more control over your life and the emotions you face.

Contrary to general beliefs, you have no control over your emotions until you regain them. The only way to control them is to accept them because then you can release them. This is the secret you can do to improve your profession as a lawyer and make your personal life a long line of pleasant experiences. Stop forcing yourself, allow your emotions to exist and release them, to find out the key to happiness. The better you become at this, the more you will enjoy your life and your work.

The better you are at releasing your emotions, the happier you will be. It is essential to learn relaxation exercises. In the face of stressful situations in life, you should know the art of relaxation. Understanding this means you have the ability to relax in any circumstance. Like any other activity in life, practice leads to perfection. One of the best relaxation exercises involves breathing. You can start with 5 minutes and gradually work up to 15 minutes. Perform this exercise at least 2-3 times a day.

Breathing and relaxation exercises

Start by laying comfortably on your back. If you prefer a sitting position, it is OK too. Put your hands on your stomach. Concentrate on your body and relax all your muscles starting from your feet, systematically, until you reach the top of your head. Once your whole body is relaxed, visualize your body as a balloon filled with air from which, with the release of the air, you release all the tension. Get in touch with your muscles and tell them to relax, you will feel your body getting heavy and sleepy. Repeat the following sentence: "I am heavy and sleepy." Observe your body as it inhales and exhales. When you inhale, you say, "Inhale," and when you exhale, you say, "Exhale."

Continue doing this exercise for 8-10 minutes (you can set an alarm if you want). Performing this exercise twice a day will create, in 4 weeks, new pathways in the body that will help you relax more easily in any situation and should be carried out regularly. We also offer you the opportunity to learn additional relaxation meditations on the eLAWvation platform (www.elawvation.com), which can guide you every time you need it.

Another effective method is Jacobson's ***Progressive Relaxation***[1].

Relax while sitting or lying down but read this exercise rigorously before you perform it. You will start to relax from your feet up. Strain your muscles for 10 seconds, then release them and relax for 10 seconds. You will move, ascending through your entire body, starting from your feet, straining and relaxing each group of muscles for 10 consecutive seconds. As you continue, you will add a group of muscles to the previous group you have strained and relaxed. Until you reach your neck, you will be tensing your entire body – neck, shoulders, back, stomach, legs and toes. Wait 10 seconds, also holding your breath, then release the muscles and relax. You will feel your whole

1 Edmund Jacobson (1888-1983) was an American medical doctor specialized in internal medicine, psychiatry and physiology, the creator of Progressive Muscle Relaxation and of Biofeedback.

body relaxed, heavy and lazy. Enjoy relaxation for another 15 minutes. This is a great exercise before going to bed.

These two exercises will give you a start to eliminate stress from your life. We hope that you will consider our suggestions and that you will do so to give both your body and your mind a needed break.

Make time to reconnect. Remember that we are consumers and energy generators. We have to keep the balance in this energy flow. When we talk about performance, we think first of all of practicing. To improve, we must train. We regenerate the resources we need to work optimally.

The extended office schedule, studio hours and overload are specific to lawyers. But no one teaches us in college or during our internship that we need to reload our batteries in order to produce. We know cases of lawyers who died because of the overload. Only when you allow yourself to devote those precious moments to self-regeneration, only then will you fully understand the importance of this subject.

Andreea: *Each person has his/her own style to relax. For me, for instance, music is important. When I'm working on a contract, when I have to draft an important act that requires my maximum concentration, background music stimulates me and relaxes me at the same time. Think about what helps you and respect yourself.*

Planning. Focus. Efficiency.

Lawyers are known to be busy and stay at the office long hours. This is because, after their activity in court, they arrive at the office late in the day and stay to begin their day's work. Most of the time, this is after 4:00 pm. How you manage meetings with potential clients, study for your cases, make time for the reports you have to do, and for the bills you need to calculate must be prioritized carefully! You should prioritize them objectively in accordance with your values.

Plan

It is normal for a lawyer to see the big picture while paying attention to the details, which are very important. Get used to making lists of priorities and important tasks every day. Allocate a specific amount of time to handle unforeseen emergencies that often appear.

We know a lot of people who are masters at wasting time at the office and that's because of a lack of focus. The main reason may be the phone. There is nothing wrong with saying "I'll call you back." We know this may seem impossible, but you don't have to do it until you know you need to focus. If you want to give maximum yield, be 100% present. Concentrate and be effective.

Pareto's principle tells us that 80% of the results are due to 20% of the time allotted. The same thing works in relation to your clients: 80% of revenue is due to contacts with 20% of clients.

But do not think that the changes we are suggesting requires extra work. It is about focusing resources not about increasing effort. If you consider the big goal, namely your intention (desire for success) – you will definitely get the desired result.

Time is still a resource to be considered when we determine the important things for us and our priorities. There are situations where you are forced to devote time to things that don't seem important to you but be careful what perspective you are thinking of. Appearances can deceive.

Alina: *Many times, meeting with potential clients exhausted me. I have a practical and results-oriented nature, so I thought it was a waste of time, especially when I had to listen to all their stories. But that time was actually an investment to establish a relationship with the people in question. I'm also a very curious person. Therefore, when I enter the heart of the problem, I get involved and the impatience disappears.*

But what can be the source of impatience in our case? There is a difference between being oriented towards the concrete outcome for you

– namely billing – and the impatience that your passion arouses for the case itself. In any situation there must be a balance. If you are used to moving quickly to action, getting started by studying, focusing and finding the solution, you're going to have to try to tame your impatience. This is for the good of your business and your reputation.

But how do you get new cases if you do not devote time to listening and developing a consistent relationship with potential clients? The competition is so huge, that no matter how good you are, the harder it is to get clients through the door without doing anything. But if you are well organized and you know from the beginning that the time allotted for this purpose has a precise role and you see it as an investment, you can relax and be present in each case.

Here is a useful exercise. We invite you to notice that when you are 100% present and you are dedicated to the discussion; you are much more appreciated. Then you will realize the other elements of communication that help you effectively lead the discussion. We wonder now how effective we would have been back then if we had these tools at the beginning of our careers. But nothing is random. We probably would not have written these books. Each person has a different path and is guided by its uniqueness. Use your uniqueness and don't distort it with the passage of time.

An effective time management tool is the creation of a list for awareness of the importance of your tasks so that you can focus your efforts in the desired direction.

Make a list of four categories:
- What is important and urgent?
- What is important but not urgent?
- What is urgent but not important?
- What is not important, and not urgent?

Make this list daily and write down every task you have to do, ticking off what you have already done.

For example:

In the category **important and urgent**: draft a greeting for the term dated.

In the category **important but not urgent**, you can enter that time dedicated to the discussion with a potential client.

In the **urgent, but unimportant** category, it can be answering an email that could be delegated to someone else.

In the **not urgent, nor important** section, enter those phone interruptions, articles read on the internet that take away your focus when looking for something important.

After you have made this planning list, observe what you have checked and, after a few days, compare the lists and observe how you managed the time, where and how unnecessary time is taking place. Now acknowledge the time wasters and make different choices when it comes to time management. Do long-term and short-term planning. If necessary, plan your time in sections, such as time for study, for socialization, for work, etc.

Remember, in all these aspects, the constant goal is balance. Don't be scared, you will have time for everything. It just seems complicated, but you will notice how you get to work differently when you dedicate time and planning. The most appropriate time to do this is at the end of the day. After this habit becomes part of your routine, you will be more relaxed and you will be able to ascertain, with surprise, the *dilation* (expansion) of time. You are going to experience the beautiful sensation of having, all of a sudden, more time.

We have all felt the pressure caused by the lack of time. We sometimes say, *"I don't have time"*, before we think about what is involved in a certain action and what is important to us. At some point, this attitude can turn into a habit and you wake up automatically saying *"I don't have time"*, although you feel like you are not effective and have no satisfaction. What can you do then? Detach from the herd and be different. Allow yourself to stop time and observe where you are at that point. Realize you are unique, and do not compare yourself to others.

Discipline and organization

Discipline does not work without organization and vice versa. For a lawyer, order is as important as breathing. Many times, you may seem to be working hard and not getting results. The loss of time for a lawyer is a sensitive subject, especially for those who are working on deadlines. Frustrations are very high in these situations, which is why we have strived, in this book, to dedicate more sections to time management.

Set your goals and be aware of your role in relation to clients. You can't ask of others what you don't deliver. You need to know where you want to go, to be clear of your desired outcome. Have you thought about how you want to be perceived by your clients? If so, then act accordingly. Your image matters. Organize your office in accordance with your goals and values. The way you organize yourself determines the results you will have.

Many reasons for frustration can occur. There's no point in asking yourself, "*Why is this happening to me but not someone else?*" Whether you work independently or in a law firm, clearly establish what your duties are, what you have to do and what is important to you depending on your goals during that period.

Establish your personal goals from the beginning and, if you work with other people, clearly define from the beginning what role each person has. Eliminate confusion about client expectations. Define what your boundaries are and delegate. Notice whether your company or your collaborators have the same goals and if their values are aligned with yours. Do not ask for what is not in accord with your values and do not forget to consider them.

We had several lawyers working for us, and our requests surpassed their ability and rhythm. Don't forget the number one value of a Unique Lawyer: the balance between personal and professional life. For us there was no balance. We were organized and efficient, but we could not rely on the others to share our values and work style. This is why it is important that if you work for someone, make sure there are common points and values.

It's up to you how you organize your life but take our word for it, when you have a plan and you are organized, things go much smoother.

In contrast, when you do not have a clear direction, maybe you will get where you are going, but you will feel exhausted and you will not be able to enjoy the results. We do not think that is your objective. So, start by organizing your life and then organize your work environment.

At our coaching sessions with lawyers, one of the most important topics is lack of time and organization. After we establish what their goals are, through coaching techniques, we help them achieve their goals easier and faster. Surely you must have a landmark to know when you have reached your goal. Consider that all your goals have a constant. Don't forget you are not alone on your journey. Without your clients you cannot grow professionally.

How do you manage a busy week?

To achieve maximum efficiency throughout the week, it is essential to work in uninterrupted periods of time, without constant distractions from emails and phone calls. We recommend that you take a little break once in a while in order to detach from all of those pressing situations in your professional activity. Short breaks, even very short ones, boost your energy levels efficiently, make you more productive and maintain low stress levels.

It is important to harmoniously combine intense periods of work with breaks. That way, you can spend shorter amounts of time at work.

Learn more about time management. Many lawyers choose to take time management courses, and this can be very useful. We have organized and will present time management courses.

Andreea: *The first time I heard about something like this, I thought it was absurd. I couldn't admit that someone could teach me how to manage my own time. Well, I want to tell you that it was one of the most important and useful courses I've ever taken. Why? First of all, because I realized how important time is, how much time I was wasting every day because I didn't know how to prioritize my life and my activities. Now, things are different because I learned how to take control.*

Each person has a mental scheme of their own, based on certain habits. Repeated behaviors shape the daily routine, especially when we are engaged in various professional activities. Become aware of the fact that every day is different, and that change can occur right now in your life. Choose to think differently to have different results.

Tips to Take Full Advantage of Every Day

Time factor

The way you handle time can make your career flourish or, it can tarnish the satisfaction of running your own business. Time management is essential for a satisfactory life, both at work and at home. It's important to efficiently manage your time and avoid wasting it. The internet, emails, and messages can distract you and make you lose many productive hours. And it adds to the accumulation of stress.

Time determines your life. In one day, there is only 24 hours. This means 1440 minutes or 86400 seconds. On a regular day, 60 to 100 minutes (6000 seconds) are easily wasted. If you are under pressure to perform, knowing this can make a difference.

We want to share some tips and techniques that can help you cope with the challenges of managing time. Maybe you will find them useful. Time management can always be improved. Your time means your life. Every second that passes means a second lost forever. Using your organizational skills, you can reduce stress and work more efficiently. Being organized does not necessarily mean being meticulous or a perfectionist. It means being able to use time in a much more useful way.

Well-organized people work more efficiently while saving time, which enables them to spend more time at home with family or simply enjoying their free time, doing what they enjoy.

Telephone

The time that you have allocated to projects often seems to go too quickly when you are frequently interrupted to answer the phone. What can you do in this case? We think a good idea would be to purchase a hands-free headset so you can continue working on other tasks while you're on the phone. The action of holding the phone between your ear and your shoulder can often create neck problems. Set an alarm for 3 minutes and try to solve each call within this timeframe. When someone calls and asks if you have a little free time, you can be brief, warning your interlocutor at the other end of the phoneline that you have only 3 minutes.

In time, what do you expect in court?

Of course, you can try to relax. Or, if you already feel "plugged in", you can try to use this time to optimize your work further. Check your to-do list. Check your emails, get organized. Delegate. Put stamps on any correspondence that is going out of the office, prepare bank transfers, scan your emails or messages and mark the important passages.

Cleaning the office

Make sure you always clean off your desk before you go home. This should not take more than 15 minutes. At the end of the week it may take longer but think how frustrating it is to find a cluttered desk on Monday morning.

Organize your work by category:

Things to be done can be placed in a box in plain sight or in a folder.

Things to be archived can be placed in a storage box.

Things to be discussed can be placed in a box marked for "discussions".

Everything you need to follow up on can be noted in your schedule.

After spending time away from the office

Upon returning from a trip, we recommend that you divide your activities into 3 categories:

High priority: Things that need your immediate attention.

Average priority: Things you need to resolve in 1 to 3 days.

Low priority: Things that can wait until you finish with the first two categories.

As soon as you have divided your work in this way, you should check your correspondence in the "high priority" category. The rest can be solved during the week.

Save time

When you are very busy, reject any new tasks. Plan meetings in other offices so you can leave when you want. Prepare a list of what you need to discuss and plan time for each item on the list. Transfer most of the incoming phone calls.

Maintain phone calls, short and to the point, and write down important points in the discussion. Limit your interruptions. Plan the moment when you think you will be free to provide an answer and convey them clearly to your colleagues. You can do relaxation and breathing exercises even while you are engaged in a telephone conversation.

Unsolicited emails (Spam)

Unsolicited emails represent a huge loss of time and concentration. Tips to save your time in this case:

- Create a new email address for shopping. This will keep your business address safe from unwanted emails.
- Never respond to spam. Responding to a spam message means that you have. confirmed your email address and you will receive more and more unwanted emails.
- Unsubscribe your email address from unwanted newsletters.
- Never open an email from an anonymous sender. Install filters for spam.

Give up excuses

Finally, we have some advice for those who seek excuses not to be organized.

Problem: *I don't have time to be organized or clean my office.*
Solution: *Schedule 15 minutes every day to organize your desk. While taking calls, you can start cleaning up the box of things you*

have to do. After a week, you will start noticing the results and feel motivated to continue.

Problem: *The pile is too big. I don't know where to start.*
Solution: *Take care of each pile one at a time. Schedule some extra hours to organize. Make a box with only priority materials and recycle the rest.*

Problem: *This is my system. That's how I know where everything is.*
Solution: *This is denial. It is important to take a step back and realize that if you become more organized, it will increase the quality of your life.*

The choice is yours. If you choose to deny there is a problem, then so be it. But remember that the chaos around you is actually the mirror of chaos in your mind.

Morning Awakening — a vital moment

In the previous pages you read some recommendations on how to schedule your day before going to bed. The most important advice was not to end your day by leaving unresolved problems. Be free from the accumulated tension throughout the day. You should introduce this healthy habit into your routine, every night, because it will help you enjoy a healthy sleep. You have at your fingertips a very effective tool: The Jacobson *Progressive Relaxation Technique* (see previous chapter), or the CDs on the eLAWvation platform. An end to the reckoning at the end of the day can prove very beneficial, both for a restful sleep, as well as for a quiet beginning of the next day. We all want to be able to wake up every morning rested and energized, free from the ballast of past worries. That is why we found it useful to further focus on ways to start your day in the best way.

A healthy diet

We have already discussed nutrition: eat lightly in the morning and take your vitamins and minerals tailored to your body's needs. Never drink coffee before 11:00 a.m. and drink a lot of water to detoxify your body. In the morning, your body needs to start its engine. Therefore, the way you start your day will influence your energy and productivity for the rest of the day.

A few recommendations:

– Set your alarm an hour early and listen to one of the CDs or MP3s mentioned in this book. The most opportune moment to listen to this kind of relaxation exercise is when you are just waking up.

– Start your day with dance. Listen to your favorite music, which is impossible for you to resist dancing to. Sing and dance. Give yourself five minutes to awaken your body entirely.

– Stretching. Give yourself a few minutes to stretch your body like a cat. Make noise while you are doing it. Try touching your toes, holding your knees straight. Hold on to your ankles and touch your nose to your knees if you can. Relax your hips, your neck and your wrists, gently rotating them. You can let the music play if you like.

– Deep Breath. It is important to fill your lungs with oxygen in the morning through deep breaths. These breathing exercises clean the lower part of the lungs, replacing stagnant air with fresh air. It is best to do so in front of an open window, even in winter.

– Cold shower. In the evening it is good to take a warm and relaxing shower. In the morning, though, it is time for action so after you dance and do some stretching exercises, a quick cold shower will stimulate your blood circulation.

– Drink water. Drink one liter of water in the morning, preferably without taking a break. During the rest of the morning, drink another liter of water. This is not about quenching your thirst, but about completing the needs of the body.

– Visualize your day. Through visualization, imagine how you will interact with others and how you will face situations today. Give yourself about five minutes. See, with your mind's eye, how no one can influence your mental state in a negative way. Observe how you work joyfully and finish your day full of energy. Use all five senses.

– Gratitude and intentions. It is a good idea to start your daily schedule thinking that every day is a new chance to design in the real world what you want, learning and growing as a person. It is the best time to keep quiet for a moment and think about all those things in your life that you can say you have been blessed with. Feel gratitude for what you have: a roof over your head, clothing, a job, family, health, etc. Usually these are things that you take for granted. Think about your life and what you want it to be like. Remember your goals and intentions.

– Start your day with enthusiasm. It is not that difficult to feel enthusiastic. Think of all the things that inspire your enthusiasm. Think of all the reasons that make you happy you are alive and all the things you still want to accomplish. Visualize your multidimensional goals. Design, mentally, the way you will achieve your goals and enjoy every second.

– Select a chapter in this book and read it again. We were saying, above, that the morning is the time of day when we are loaded with energy and vitality and can take time to think of all those good things in our lives, for which we deserve to be grateful. Use today's morning to focus on the satisfaction your career offers. We recommend that you reread sections of this book, including passages you have marked, that can help you acknowledge those aspects of your daily activity that make you feel professionally accomplished. Emphasize what is important to you. This will really help you absorb the information into your neurological system.

At the end of each day

We are close to the end of this book. I congratulate you on your perseverance and motivation. We hope you have already applied some of our suggestions. We hope that we have managed to convince you how important it is to invest in yourself and to live your life as beautifully as possible. Now is the time to act, to try to implement what you have discovered. We believe that by implementing a few new habits suggested in this book, you will be able to break the old barriers and discover your uniqueness. The

Unique Lawyer System helps you to implement the information in this book, thus passing the practical level in your career.

It has always fascinated us that some people are successful, and others are not. Success is more than just performing well and obtaining a higher social status. It means doing everything you can with your life while growing spiritually.

Being "more than a lawyer". The most important rule is this: to achieve more success or to enjoy your career and personal life more, you must be open to change. This is a great challenge, because humans are creatures shaped through habits. By the time you prove yourself able to change, you will have to knock down old patterns and install new ones into your routine, for a minimum of three weeks.

Any shorter period of time will not have a lasting effect. The best results will be achieved when you take at least three weeks to implement a new pattern into your neurological system. Then you'll need another three weeks to get used to it on a mental level and another three weeks to implement it at a bioenergy level. This is the path to success and subconscious competence.

In conclusion, new habits need 3 x 3 weeks to be fully integrated into your system. The *Unique Lawyer System* has 4 modules, and each module contains 5 well-structured lessons that help you integrate all the necessary information into your nervous system to replace old habits with new habits, to make the difference in your personal life and in your professional life as well.

It is very important to break old patterns.

The most important reason people self-sabotage is the persistent old patterns. They are well-printed at the level of your neurological, mental and energetic system.

Here is an example that probably sounds familiar. You decided to wake up very early Monday morning to exercise. You set your alarm at 6 a.m. (an hour earlier than normal). The alarm is triggered at the scheduled time. Your nervous system is used to waking up at 7 a.m. You are neurologically programmed to wake up an hour later, so to be active at 6 a.m.

may prove difficult. Even if you manage to get out of bed, you are going to have a confrontation with your mental system. This system will come up with all kinds of excuses: *"It's a bad idea to be active at this hour", "It's too cold, too dark", "I need my sleep..."*

If you manage to ignore this programming, thanks to your willpower, you will be able to change your psychic programming. It is no wonder that many people will not be able to get out of bed or that they will return in a week to their old habits. An important part of destroying old patterns is to prepare by starting the evening before. That means going through every step, in detail, through visualization. Many performance athletes are known for visualizing their victories before, living, in their mind's eye, every second of their accomplishment on the road to success. Try to visualize your victories first.

The view is related to the programming of the neurological system. The brain cannot distinguish between images and reality. The same number of neurons is activated during visualization as during the realization of the act itself, provided we use multidimensional visualization. That means using our senses: sight, taste, touch, smell and hearing. You have to imagine what it looks like, what it tastes like, how it feels, how it smells, and what it sounds like for your new habits that you want to implement. Use the relaxation techniques discussed earlier. Scan your body, search for voltage outbreaks and free yourself from them, then continue your visualization exercise.

Visualization example

Imagine that a client starts yelling at you, telling you how unskilled you are, and that you are to blame for his loss. Visualize how you can stay calm. You will notice his nostrils flaring and you will find it amusing. You feel relaxed and you can easily understand how unhappy and tense he is. Perhaps something saddens him in his existence. Maybe he made an unfortunate choice, or he is in a situation he doesn't want to be in. You feel sorry for him, because he is talented, but he cannot get into his role. You see him breaking and coming out of the office leaving behind just dust. This is a multidimensional view.

In this visualization you see your own answers and experience the release of the tension that your client's uncomfortable presence is causing you. Performing such exercises every day reprograms your neurological system. Eventually, what you see in your mind will happen in reality. You can see yourself going to the office with enthusiasm and coming back after a long day of work. You can also see yourself spending more time with your family.

You can imagine past events, which you would have liked to have performed differently. For example, let's say you had an argument with a colleague, and you told him something that you now regret. You felt bad at the time, but you avoided apologizing. Our ego can be stubborn. Viewing the moment in which you apologize or even changing the entire course of the conversation can change the way you feel and can help you relieve your tension.

Another example: Your boss is continuously in a bad mood and you do not want to let him affect you anymore. Every time he screams at you, he hurts your feelings. That makes you nervous and angry, so you feel very tense at work. You would like to change that. How is that going to happen?

In the evening, in bed, you visualize how you want things to go. Your answer to the aggressive boss's attitude is to stay calm. You can change your own response, but not the other person's. You will visualize your answer as being one of calm acceptance when your boss yells at you. Investigate the real problem and do not take it personally. His disproportionate reaction has nothing to do with you. You stay relaxed. That way you can continue your work completely untouched.

Visualization is able to create your own reality, as you would like to see it in real life. It is an easy exercise to do and requires only 5-10 minutes a day. Never go to bed with unsolved problems or full of tension. This harmful habit can kidnap your restful sleep. Procrastination is done at your own expense because, sooner or later, you have to confront those things, so you better do it right away.

From now on you can find yourself in a virtuous circle.

CHAPTER 5

You are the expert in yourself!

We only helped you to discover it...

Chapter 5
Conclusion

The Unique Lawyer System

Our four modules are specifically designed to come to the aid of those lawyers who want to make a difference and know that they have to invest in their personal development, and wan to elevate their professional career and personal life.

Lawyers can use the Unique Lawyer system

- After experience in a law firm, they want to start an individual practice. In this way, they can achieve their goals faster and much easier.
- Throughout all stages of their law practice, they wish to overcome their limitations,
- For example, they want to learn a more effective strategy for their own promotion.
- Established lawyers can use the Unique Lawyer system to develop leadership skills within the organizations they are involved in.
- Law firms use the system to streamline their communication and business growth.
- Many lawyers with extensive experience and practice use the system to face changes in the market, to improve their skills, to develop strategies adapted to the new requirements and to refresh their enthusiasm towards the practice of their profession.
- To improve your management practices.

We would like this book to represent for our readers the first step of their long journey to success, which we perceive in its multifunctional dimension as a common denominator of both personal and professional life.

We wanted to first offer our peers (but not only them) more than a book. Therefore, we used this means of communication as an interface for the method we designed in the *Unique Lawyer System*. We have worked extensively with a set of tools and strategies that we strongly believe can help you in your dream of ranking in the top elite attorneys. This is essentially the purpose for which we created the *Unique Lawyer System*: To propel yourself to the top, where you can make a difference in the lives of those around you, but also for humankind in general. With your uniqueness, consciousness, that which defines you, by excellence.

We know it takes courage to find or redefine your identity in a world blazed and numbed by routine and superficiality. That is why we are here to support you, not only by sharing the ideas that are found in this book, but also through the platform that we created, the *Unique Lawyer System* (www.elawvation.com), through the courses that we designed, and through the coaching sessions we provide for lawyers. Together we want to win the case of our life, gaining harmony in our own lives and in relation to our clients.

We realized, after years of experience in this field, that the unit of measure of the value of a lawyer is given by his personal sacrifice. But for the Unique Lawyer, this sacrifice is sacred, because he does not give up his own aspirations, principles or even his own health and wellbeing by virtue of winning the cause of his client. Unique Lawyers become creators in relation to the interpretation of the law in their professional role.

But there are other dimensions of sacrifice in the professional trajectory of the Unique Lawyer. It is about his successive and continuous endeavors in the sense of perfection, of often passionate involvement in several spheres of existence and in several areas of knowledge, all in order to become a valuable support point for his clients and a guarantor of respect for law.

The lawyer's vocation must be multidimensional. Like the ancient Proteus – *God Marin gifted by Poseidon with the gift of prophecy, who had the power to morph into fire, earth, water or in animal dives, to evade questions posed by mortals* – we are challenged to wear different hats, thus we juggle with areas of the most diverse clients, and adapt our communication style according to the people we work with. Besides, we always have to deal with different people, with different cases, so we have to show a great availability to act in unforeseen situations, we must be prepared to act in front of unpredictable situations and be open to unprecedented paths. To be creative and, at the same time, understanding with the many facets of uniqueness of each person and each situation.

We believe that this book can prove a useful guide to those lawyers who want to discover the skills necessary for the harmonious conduct of their activity, without losing themselves in the process. There was a moment in our long journey to personal success when we found ourselves near the edge of the cliff, risking losing ourselves. We considered our experience as an alarm signal for our colleagues, many of whom were at the beginning of the road. We therefore considered the positive and negative part of our professional experience and mixed them in this book that aims to ease the work of lawyers but, in particular, to help them find joy and enthusiasm in practicing this profession. We would like the Unique Lawyer in the future to see in it as more than just a profession, so as he will actually manage to be more than a lawyer...

From lawyers to lawyers, made with love.
Enjoy your journey, Alina & Andreea

Thanks

Thank God for everything.

We thank our parents who have contributed to our lives each with a unique and different gift.

We would like to thank all the people in our lives who have contributed to whom we are today.

Thank you to everyone with whom we have collaborated on The Unique Lawyer project.

This is not an end; this is a start; ours and yours.

So, we put our mother's words here--who represents our openness to the world that I have spoken so fondly about in this book.

God gave me a wonderful gift: twins girls. He listened to my wish.

They grew up, studied, were loving, were struggling. They learned at the school of life. And, they have accomplished everything with the power of their hearts, intelligence of humanity and the desire of beauty and good. Hope this book to help every reader to make a difference in personal and professional life.

Author's Mother, Maria Nicolae

www.elawvation.com

Made in the USA
Las Vegas, NV
03 November 2026

57420895R00133